Startled *by* Silence

STARTLED *by* SILENCE

Finding God in Unexpected Places

Ruth Senter

Zondervan Publishing House
Grand Rapids, Michigan

Daybreak Books are published by Zondervan Publishing House,
1415 Lake Drive, S.E., Grand Rapids, Michigan 49506.

Library of Congress Cataloging in Publication Data

Senter, Ruth Hollinger, 1944-
Startled by silence.

"Daybreak Books."
1. Meditations. I. Title.
BV4832.2.S45 1986 242 85-22542

ISBN 0-310-38840-6

Edited and designed by Julie Ackerman Link

Printed in the United States of America

86 87 88 89 90 91 / 10 9 8 7 6 5 4 3 2 1

Against the Word the unstilled world still whirled
About the center of the silent Word.
    O my people, what have I done unto thee.
Where shall the word be found, where will the word
Resound? Not here, there is not enough silence.

—From *Ash-Wednesday*
by T. S. Eliot

Contents

Come with me
Listen to the ordinary detail of your life
Words not yet written
Stories yet untold
Empty spaces
Blank pages
Pictures not yet painted.

They are there
If you will
Pay attention
To the silence
Observe carefully
Your space.
For it
Has spoken
Is speaking
Will speak
If you will
Listen
Learn
And write your own pages.

PART I: WHEN GOD SEEMS SILENT . . . SILENCE SPEAKS

CHAPTER ONE

Unanswered Questions

What Do You Say?

What do you say when the winds of
prejudice rip across your accomplishments
and scatter them like dried leaves in a
hurricane?
When someone else's insecurity plays
havoc with your personal comfort
because they:
misunderstand your actions,
misrepresent your position,
misread your statements?

No open-mindedness.
No questions asked.
just opinions of steel—
opinions set to destroy.

What do you say when you're the victim of
political power plays that toss you from
one judge to another?
Put you on trial when there's been
no offense,
pronounce you guilty without hearing
your side.
No justice.
No fairness.
just cold, crass politics—
to keep the power-wielders happy.

What do you say when the people you
trust most let you down in your
crisis hour?
When they:

Sleep through the tensions
going on inside you,
sell you down the river for
their own personal profit,
slip out the side door and
leave you standing alone?

No sensitivity.
No empathy.
Just preoccupation with
their own safety and
comfort.

What do you say when you've been
Beaten by the system,
Stripped because of its
intolerance,
Nailed down because you don't
uphold the system's
interpretation of the truth?
Placed under lock and key because
it fears its own weaknesses?

What do you say?

Then they led Him to the place
called The Skull;
Executed Him among criminals.
And He said:
"Father, forgive them; for they know
not what they do."

(Luke 23:34)

God of the Jigsaw

"Don't try to figure me out, just love me," I said to Mark one day as he shook his head at me in absolute bewilderment. The cause of his perplexity has long since been forgotten, but the statement lives on.

I thought of it again when I read about how God dealt with the Israelites for worshiping the golden calf: "Go back and forth through the camp from one end to the other, each killing his brother and friend and neighbor" (Exodus 32:27). The Lord God of Israel said this to His people.

Harsh! Heartless! Cruel! I wanted to scream to my God of love, "*Where is Your mercy, Your forgiveness, Your grace?*"

I wanted to shout it again when I followed the coffin of a four-year-old neighbor; felt the slow, steady pulse of pain in my back; held the hand of a young widow left with two small children. Instead I simply shook my head in bewilderment, unable to understand an all-powerful God who, with a single gesture, can roll out the universe but who, when it comes to the lives of His children, sometimes appears not to lift a hand.

But I am not destroyed by God's mysterious ways. Here lies the foundation of my trust: I don't have to *understand* to *love*. To reduce God to a $5.98 jigsaw puzzle that I can put together, each piece in perfect place, would cheapen Him. It would reduce Him to my level.

In a world where we still must follow small coffins to cemeteries, we will never be able to understand or explain the enigma of a Man who lived thirty-three years in order to die; of a blinding light that revitalized body cells grown cold over three days, rolled a boulder from a cave, and conquered death once and for all.

I do not understand. But God is not diminished by my inability to reduce Him to a formula or to put Him together like a puzzle.

In fact, He wouldn't *be* God if He could be captured, contained, or perfectly understood (Isaiah 55:8). He would be mortal—and I could not give my life, my loyalty, my unreserved allegiance to anyone as finite as myself.

It is His mystery that inspires me to worship, to explore His depths, and to confess that I can't always fit together the pieces of His ways. There are times, through the silence, when I can almost hear Him say, "Ruth, don't try to figure Me out. Just love Me."

Looking Away

He stood alone in a sheltered spot where two walls came together, his hands in his pockets, his slanted eyes staring blankly into nothing. I looked twice. Who was he and what was he doing here at this time of the morning?

"You need some help?"

I could see the whites of his eyes as he looked my direction. He nodded and with the back of his hand wiped the saliva that was seeping form his mouth. I wanted to turn away but I knew I was already committed.

"Let's see if we can't find your class." I took his short, stubby hand and guided him down the hall.

He's all wrong, I thought to myself as we walked together. *So obviously wrong. A head that is way too small for his body. A nose that is too flat. Ears and teeth that are not the right size. Eyes slanted in the wrong direction.*

Rounding the corner into Wing B, we met my friend

Sue. Her eyes did a quick scan of my companion, then she looked the other way. She never even saw I was there. I opened my mouth to speak but she was gone.

Sue had never passed by me before. We always had a million things to say to each other and never enough time to say them all. But today it was as though I were invisible.

As my companion and I continued toward the classroom for handicapped children, no one in those usually friendly halls showed any signs of recognizing me. I was baffled. These were the halls of my church. People always talked to me.

Then it struck me. People weren't seeing me because of the mongoloid child at my side. Did distorted bodies make them so uncomfortable that they had to turn the other direction?

"Lonely world, isn't it, little fellow?" I thought to myself as I patted him on the head and delivered him safely to his teacher.

My walk down the hall with a mongoloid child didn't end that day—at least not in my mind. I realized that except for my curiosity and noble feelings that prompted me to be a Good Samaritan, I too would have looked the other way.

I've done it much of my life: the time a man in front of me at church had an epileptic convulsion; when my brother fell on a rock and ripped his head wide open; and when I walked among the grotesque forms of humanity that slumped over brown bottles in the streets of New York's Bowery.

I would rather life didn't paint such unattractive pictures. I prefer happiness and normalcy. I would rather not see a man without legs or a woman with a hole in her throat and a tube sticking out so she can talk. I prefer not to have to stand by a casket and face the cold, lifeless body of my four-year-old neighbor who used to run through our front yard and swing on our porch swing.

Although God does not hold me responsible for figuring out the reasons for life's distortions, I am responsible for how I respond to them, because Jesus taught me the correct response. He did not turn off the ugly side of life or look the other way. He didn't go into hibernation, indifferent to suffering people. Instead, he reached out and touched people's abnormalities. He gave sanity to a boy with an evil spirit who lay on the ground foaming at the mouth and slashing himself with stones. He placed his hands on a leper—His society's most abhorred outcasts—and pronounced him clean. He took Jairus's dead daughter by the hand and said, "My child, get up." Jesus touched the most ugly sores of humanity and used His power to change them.

I didn't change anything about the little mongoloid boy that Sunday morning when I helped him find his room. He will probably drool and roll his eyes all his life. His head will never get any larger nor his nose any longer. But perhaps my silent act of taking his wet, stubby hand in mine somehow said to him, "You are a valuable and special part of God's world. I can no longer afford to look the other way."

Beyond the Superficial

"Why don't they get that kid's eyes fixed. Don't his parents realize he hasn't got a chance looking like that?"

I winced at the stranger's thoughtless words. That was my *friend* she was talking about. Lovable, huggable, four-year-old Jonathan. Every time he saw me, he called out, "Root! Root! Can I come to your house today?" Then he'd shuffle toward me, his little body leaning too far to one side, and reach out for me. His brown eyes were always smiling. I'd stoop down and hug him, hoping somehow he could feel my squeeze through the hard plastic brace that had housed his body since he was fourteen months old.

I looked at his mother and hoped she hadn't heard. She was patiently coaching Jonathan's little hands as they struggled for control while ice cream trickled down his chin. She had been his patient coach since the doctors shook their heads years before. They extended their sympathy after using such frightening terms as cerebral palsy, severe mental retardation, hypotonic, no muscle control, institutionalization.

The fight to overcome had been long and hard. Jonathan's mother had met all the obstacles with courage. The fact that her son walked and talked at all was a monument to her patience and perseverance.

But no one asked about Jonathan's mother's courage today. No one spoke of the hope that had sustained her through the dark months of hurt and disappointment. No one seemed to care how it felt to wipe melting ice cream off your son's chin while other boys his age quickly gobbled up every bit of the cool refreshment, refusing to leave even a drop on their chins or in the cone, and then tore off to ride their bicycles down narrow sidewalks or to skip lightly over cracks in the sidewalk.

No one seemed to wonder, either, what life was like for my little friend. They never got beyond his eyes.

I thought that day of the One who is far less concerned with what is outside than He is with what is *inside.* Jesus Christ looks beyond the superficial. He is much more aware of how people feel than how they look.

One day He saw emptiness. He didn't mind that it resided in the heart of a Samaritan woman, who Jewish religious leaders refused to even look upon. Jesus, uninhibited by their prejudices, stopped, talked, and ministered to her need. The woman was surprised; so were His disciples (John 4:9, 27). But externals didn't matter to God's Son. No wonder people were healed by His touch.

I walked over and held Jonathan's little hand, still sticky from the ice cream. His large brown eyes smiled up at me. Funny, I'd forgotten that his eyes were crossed.

The Misfit

His life goes out with a bang.
The crowds gather
Spectators cheer
And death hawks its wares.
Cheap flesh
A common criminal
Small town boy
With grand illusions
And lofty dreams about his own identity.
Society has a place for people who lose touch with reality.
White coats
Black robes
Iron bars
Unstained wood that drips blood.
And so "The Misfit" meets his final foe
Surrenders up his soul
And dies.
Conquered
Contained

UNANSWERED QUESTIONS

Put in his place.
In the west the sun sets
And darkness disperses the crowd.
But in this place of dead-men's bones
The earth groans with the weight that it
bears
A form unfit for death
Designed for life.
The rocks cry out
They roll away.
Concrete slabs split in two
While the earth rejects what it cannot
rightfully keep.
Nature reverses its flow
rids itself of its terrible crime.

"The Misfit" shakes eternity.
For every eye shall see
Every knee shall bow.
And in the east, The Son rises
And His rays light the whole world.

Why Pray?

Surely God already knows what He's going to do with my life, so why should I pray? Within the split second it took the heavy-duty utility truck to plow past the yield sign and into my path—brakes screeching, metal interlocking, and glass flying—I knew I'd found my answer.

Just twenty-four hours earlier I had said good-bye to a group of new friends in Seattle and had boarded a plane for home. We had been together for three days in the peaceful fir country west of Puget Sound.

Most of us met as strangers at that retreat. We had prayed together in small groups, not because we felt any great need but because the schedule called for it. In the beginning no one said much. Polite formalities only, nothing private or personal.

But over steaming cups of tea and homemade cinnamon rolls, we laid aside our façades. We walked together down quiet paths among the giant firs and left behind our concerns about what others might think.

Against the green of the forest or along streams of blue, hurts emerged. Pain—some old, some new—was expressed. Disappointments of yesterday. Hopes for tomorrow. Gradually we began to catch sight of the people behind the faces.

In the end, we didn't have enough hours to say it all. As we joined hands and formed a prayer pact, we promised to pray especially for each other during the following twenty-four hours.

My friends gathered around me for a final farewell. "Lord," one prayed, "during this next day, put Your wall of protection around Ruth. We know the lows often come just after the highs. Keep Ruth—mentally, physically, and spiritually—during these next twenty-four hours."

We hugged each other, waved a final good-bye, and I began the long flight home.

My plane lifted off at 1:05 on Wednesday afternoon. Thursday afternoon, just before the twenty-four-hour period ended, the utility truck plowed through the yield sign, nearly totaling my car. I walked away with bruises and an aching back.

Why pray? Because the schedule calls for it—prayer is an act of obedience. Sometimes, even when friends pray, utility truck drivers fail to yield the right of way. I am not responsible for the results of prayer. I am only responsible to obey. Why pray? I'm not sure, except God tells me to. And for me, that's reason enough.

Listen to the unanswered questions in your life.
What do you hear?

CHAPTER TWO

Life and Death

God Is So Good?

Yesterday was tangle-free.
My day was peaceful and predictable.
Consistent with a God of love,
The birds sang,
The sun shone,
The children obeyed.
My neighbor across the street extended her Christianity to me with a loaf of bread still warm from her oven.
And I
Hugged my children,
Opened my arms wide to the sun,
Bit deeply into the freshness of rye and melted butter.
Aloud I said, "God is so good."

That was yesterday.
Today I stumble in a tangled web of confusion and disorder.
Jori met me at the front door with the staggering message: "Mom, Katherine died."
My friend Katherine—
one of my partners in Tuesday morning Bible study—
dead!
My brain staggered with the weighty information.
I had no place to put it.
No mental file designated
"Death of a friend;
mother of a twenty-four-hour-old infant."
Suddenly I am a stranger in my own house,
lost in my own kitchen.
It doesn't fit. It just doesn't fit!
The birth was so ordinary. So easy.

Why the sudden headache? Why the coma?
Why the death at all?
Why? Why? Why?
I move through the reality of Katherine's death—
a tangled jumble of emotions, physical symptoms, questions.

God is good?

I look at the newborn, asleep in his motherless room.
I reach out and take the hand of the grieving father.
"I'm so sorry. Katherine was a special person."
I tell him about the rainy morning she called me.
"You have a lot to do for the brunch," she had said.
"Let me come early and help you get ready."
For a moment her husband and I are bound together
in the happy memory of when Katherine was with us.
I leave my basket of fruit and cheese on the kitchen table
and slip out the side door.
Katherine's two older boys are coming home from the neighbor's.
The three-year-old clutches a stuffed puppy in his arms.
His five-year-old brother walks by me with his eyes lowered.

God is good?

Three motherless boys.
An empty rocking chair.
A daddy alone.
I drive home wondering. I feel knots inside and out.
At last I say aloud, "Yes, God is still good.
I have no alternative but to believe Him.
Even when I can't understand."

Warm Days and Tombstones

The day had a life and death irony about it. Warm June sun and stone-cold concrete. Bursts of new life—petunias, geraniums, and lilies-of-the-valley—marking the passing of the seasons. Final epitaphs—names, dates, and family links—marking the passing of the generations.

"Mellinger's Mennonite Church." We slowed the car as we approached the sign and turned right into the parking lot. For my mother, this place was not only a house of God but also a house of childhood memories. In a sense, she was home. Cradled on the grassy slopes that surrounded the old, red brick structure were her people: the Diffenbaughs, the Martins, the Goods, the Mellingers. We moved among the memories of flesh and blood; among names I knew from the Old German Family Bible on Mother's coffee table at home. I reached down and touched the marble, rubbed my hand over block letters smoothed by time. She only lived to be twenty-eight. She was the grandmother I had never known. Dead of tuberculosis when my mother was only four.

There was no granite and marble on the upper slopes—only summer's spread of grass, deep green arborvitae, and a sprawling oak tree or two. I felt I was walking from past into future. I knew someday I'd stand on these same slopes and touch death closeup. Someday it would no longer be the vague ancestors of another generation buried here, but those with whom I'd shared life.

"Plots 43 through 46. Right here under this oak." The cemetery caretaker stopped at the far end of the ridge. We looked down on the peaceful valley of marble and concrete.

"What a beautiful view," my mother said. She was facing the church and the gentle hills beyond. "Just right for the resurrection," my dad added. His voice was confident and calm. I watched his steady hand as he signed the contract. "Hollinger. Plots 43, 44, 45, 46." He screwed the top back on his pen, folded the paper, and put it into his portfolio for safekeeping. We had agreed on our immortality. Now we could go home.

"Only the person who is not afraid to die is the person who is not afraid to live." I thought of General MacArthur's words as we turned out of Mellinger's Cemetery and headed home. Someday Mellinger's Cemetery will be a place, not of final defeat, but of ultimate victory. Today we had taken one step toward that day of triumph.

Randy's Song

Sometimes it's hard to sing. I could tell Nicky was struggling with tears. He was singing Randy's song. In fact, all of the evening's music belonged to Randy; it was a memorial to an eight-year old classmate who had slipped beneath the dark waters of an ice-jammed lake and never again opened his eyes. Father, son, and snowmobile had been pulled from the frigid water the following day.

"Randy's dead," was all Nick said that fateful day when he walked in from school. As I gathered him into my arms, his grief came pouring out—grief that streaked his cheeks and splashed my blouse where I held him. Then words came. Slowly. Thoughtfully. Through the afternoon and on into the night.

"Randy and I were going to the pros together." We looked at the football team picture that hung on his bedroom wall. "Carol Stream Panthers, 70-Pounders, 1982." Nick and Randy stood together.

"I feel like God didn't answer my prayer. I prayed so hard that he wouldn't die . . . He was my best friend, next to Trey . . ." He straightened himself up and reached for another tissue. "I have to go and say good-bye to him on Sunday."

Now, two days after his final farewell to Randy, Nick stood and sang for his friend.

"I wish Randy was here tonight," he had said as he dressed for the evening. "Mom, why do you think God let him die?"

It was another of his questions for which I had no easy, made-to-order response. So I simply said, "Nicky, sometimes life is like looking into a mirror in a dark room. We can't see our reflection because of the dark. Someday when we see God we'll understand Randy's death."

I pointed to 1 Corinthians 13:12. "Until then," I said, "we'll just have to be content not to understand." He nodded his assent.

"I didn't really feel like singing tonight," Nick said later that evening as I tucked him into bed. "But I did it anyhow."

"And Nicky," I answered through the dark, "sometimes we *have* to sing even when we don't feel like it."

He sighed deeply. "Yep. I guess so." He turned over and hugged his pillow like he always does when he's ready for sleep.

I knew Randy's song was preparing him for life's next disappointment.

On Learning of a Friend's Terminal Cancer

The shadow
Like icy claws of dark
Oozes through the cracks
Of my spirit
Where no sunshine is.
It presses hard
Against
  Reason
  Logic
  Sense.
It makes no sense.
There is no sense
In shadows.
Only
  Fear
  Unknown
  None light.
Scary figures on the wall
Which is the darkest of them all?

ON LEARNING OF A FRIEND'S TERMINAL CANCER

"Yea though I walk . . . "
I walk through the shadow.
Hide and seek
But mostly hide.
Black and gray
But mostly black.
Life and death
But mostly death.
Through the shadow
I walk.
There is no light.
Only a Hand.

Family Reunion

August was unusually warm. It hung in hot, heavy masses and clung to our skin like a steamy comforter. Even central Pennsylvania felt like the tropics.

No one wanted to move. We sat in the shade of the front porch, drank ice lemonade, and waited for the oscillating fan to turn our way. Every ounce of energy was spent fighting the heat.

When Mother finally suggested it was time for us all to get ready for the reunion, I groaned inwardly. A conclave of the generations on a one-hundred-degree day sounded anything but appealing. Uncles. Great aunts. Grandpa's Daddy's sister. Aunt Fannie's oldest child with Grandpa's eyes. First, second, and third cousins. Faces and forms I hadn't seen for fifteen years and probably wouldn't see for another ten. What did it matter? We lived different places, went separate ways, and, except for the hereditary thread that tied us together, had very little in common.

What's so important about eating sandwiches with second cousins once removed and wiping sweat, swatting flies, and slapping mosquitoes. But here I was, sitting on a hard, backless picnic bench, swatting flies and swapping stories about the good old days.

Uncle Phares told most of the stories. For a time, I forgot the heat, flies, and mosquitoes and remembered only that he and my dad were once boys together. He pulled out his box of old black-and-white snapshots of little boys riding horses, jumping through hoops, and dressed in knickers, white shirts, and suspenders.

Next was Europe, Uncle Phares' more recent pictorial update. I eagerly leaned over the table and looked at pictures until my back ached and I thought I'd never walk straight again. But I felt as if I knew Uncle Phares. My own flesh and blood. Funny how I'd never noticed before that he looked so much like my dad.

In October mother's phone call told of Uncle Phares' death. Suddenly I was back in that one-hundred-degree meadow, in a sense, paying my final respects to Uncle Phares. It would have been easier not to go. But when you're a family you go out of your way for each other—the way God did for His family. Today, I'm very glad that on that hot August day, I did.

What Do You Say to a Dying Man?

The call I'd been expecting came today. "Art died," the church secretary said. I wasn't surprised, but now that the time had come I couldn't think of anything to say.

I thought back to an evening not long ago when Mark and I dropped by to see Art. The snow crunched under our boots and the Christmas lights winked from the front windows as we walked to the door. The house looked happy enough from the outside, but inside was the sober realization that this would probably be Art's last Christmas.

"Come on in." He greeted us cheerfully from his hospital bed in the corner of the living room. His thin hand motioned to the piano bench that was beside his bed. I couldn't help but think how often I had seen those same hands, strong and sure, bring piano keys to life. Now his baby grand sat in the corner like a slumbering giant, and his muted trumpet rested on its stand at the foot of his bed.

What do you say to a dying man? I had come with all kinds of encouraging words and ideas of things to talk about. I meant to ask about the music camp he directed last summer, the book he wrote last year, and his daughter's wedding coming up in April. I never got to my list.

"It's not easy giving up your instruments . . . kind of like saying good-bye to life-long friends . . . Rosemary's in the kitchen . . . Say hello to her . . . She's a fine woman . . . worked herself to exhaustion planning a surprise party for my fiftieth birthday last week . . . Birthdays can be traumatic . . . So is cancer . . . Hardest thing is the pain and the medication . . . makes you a stranger to yourself . . . Sometimes you have no idea why you say or do things . . . almost like you're another person . . ."

Art talked on. His words began to slow down. I could tell he was getting tired. We stood to go.

"Thanks for coming," he said. "You've been a real encouragement to me."

Mark and I squeezed his hand and said good-bye.

We encouraged him? I thought to myself as we walked to the car. *We didn't even say anything.*

Then I realized we'd *listened* rather than talked—probably the best thing we possibly could have done for a dying man.

Reason to Celebrate

Cameras scan the wide, white door decked with garlands of green, then zoom in on a fire blazing on the hearth. Silver bells and mistletoe. Joyful songs float from a baby grand piano. Happy faces gaze at the treasures piled beneath a huge spruce tree. The setting is idyllic. Mothers and fathers, grandpas and grandmas, glide through the room. Holding hands, hugging, laughing, sipping wassail from silver cups. All is bliss and happiness.

I sit in my living room watching the TV fantasy. Across the street my neighbor's lights burn into the night. Police cars come and go. Their only daughter, twenty-year-old Julie, who disappeared while en route to work, has been found five miles away. Dead of gunshot wounds . . .

"Joy to the world, the Lord is come." The sound of singing fills the halls of the nursing home. I walk through a semi-dark room and take the hand gripping a bedrail.

"Merry Christmas." Her eyes blink open for a minute or two.

"Do I know you?" Her tired face shuts down again.

"No. You don't know me. I'm just here to say 'God bless you.'" This time she groans and turns her head toward the wall where a photograph smiles down at her. The man's face looks distinguished and gentle. I wonder where he is tonight . . .

I push a buzzer and wait. Second floor, east wing is quiet on Christmas Eve. Too quiet. Through an intercom on the wall, a squeaky voice asks for my credentials. Then the thick door to the psychiatric ward swings open. I walk through in search of my friend. She is singing with the other residents of second east, "'Tis the season to be jolly."

Soon the carols end and carolers shuffle down the hall like robots. They turn into their rooms and close their doors on each other.

My friend and I sit on the edge of her bed and talk. Her speech is slow. Her mind seems to be racing to catch up. I pray with her, then leave my tray of cookies on her nightstand next to the picture of her seven-year-old. She hugs me and I see that her eyes are misty. We walk together to the end of the hall. The heavy steel door closes behind me. Tomorrow is December 25.

As I light the last candle on our advent wreath I think of Bethlehem's Child, born in the shadow of a cross. No fantasy world of silver bells and mistletoe, just the cold realities of life and death. But I celebrate anyhow. I light my candles and sing my carols because Christ has come to wrap the grim realities of life with purpose. Significance. Meaning. Reason enough to celebrate.

Listen to the life and death that touches you.
What do you hear?

CHAPTER THREE

Pain

Suffering Reconsidered

You came to me
Not in downy, soft blankets,
  White, sterile sheets,
  Or antiseptic incubator.
They didn't close Your windows
  To keep out the germs;
Spray "white lace and roses"
  To improve Your air;
Inoculate You at 18 months
  To kill potential viruses.

But You touched the earth
  Where the air hung heavy with animal waste
  And the wind blew cold between the cracks;
  Hard splinters,
  Rough, coarse hay Your bed.
You lived among splinters of wood and
  iron spikes.
But You reached for life
  Without protection.
  Drank of the dust.
  Breathed its pollution.
You moved among earth's viruses
  And touched its sores.
And when Your last great enemy, death,
Tore You from the One who loved You most,

You agonized alone.
"My God, My God, why have You forsaken Me?"
Ultimate pain—the pain of rejection.

Tonight I kneel in the garden of my own Gethsemane.
"Father, if it be possible, remove this cup from me."
But the heavens are mute.
R.S.V.P. request in a dead-letter file.
There is no answer.
Pain stalks the broken vertebra of my back
and sticks a thousand needles into my toes.
There is no relief.
I cower in the shadows of a sleepless night
In my downy, soft blankets,
White, sterile sheets,
And thermostatically-controlled air.
I reach for the doctor's prescription
To dull the pain
As I pray for deliverance.
While on a hill outside of town
Your skies remained silent;
The Father turned His back.
Pain conquered.
For a while.
Who am I to claim exemption?

Delicate Surgery

I stared straight up at the pattern in the ceiling tiles as the high-intensity lamp glared down at me. The hand at the other end of my arm seemed to belong to someone other than myself. But the clanking of instruments on sterile trays and the strong smell of alcohol reminded me that the hand the doctor was about to repair was indeed mine. I took a deep breath and braced myself for the ordeal.

"A little nervous?" Dr. Wood's voice was calm, yet concerned. "A few more minutes and you won't feel the pain." He gently probed the wreckage at the tips of my fingers. "Mean storm window, I'd say," he exclaimed. "Must have fallen hard!"

I felt he understood my hurt.

"It could have been much worse," I offered, trying to talk myself into bravery. My mind retrieved a news story

I'd read months earlier about this hospital and an eighteen-year-old whose severed hand had been reattached. It was a story of amazing skill. After ten hours of surgery and the use of a microscope that magnified small vessels to forty times their original size, the doctors had restored veins, arteries, tendons, tissues, and nerves with sutures measuring half the diameter of a human hair! Suddenly I had complete trust in the man who bent over my left hand and gently repaired the damaged ends of my fingers.

Several weeks have passed since that hospital visit, and my fingers are healing. But today as I read through Paul's letter to the church at Galatia, I was reminded again of my doctor's skill.

The word *restore* stands out on the page. "Brothers," Paul writes, "if someone is caught in a sin, you who are spiritual should *restore* him gently" (Gal. 6:1).

"Restore," I learn, is a translation of the Greek word *katartizo,* which in Paul's day was a medical term meaning "to mend" or "to set bones," an action requiring great skill.

I've read Galatians 6:1 many times before. But today for the first time I understand the gentleness, the thoughtful care, and the sensitivity to hurt that is required of me if I am to help restore a brother or sister who has stumbled over some spiritual obstacle. Spiritual pain can be just as deep as physical hurt. Both require gentle care and sensitivity for healing to occur. Dr. Wood's gentle care reminded me of my responsibility.

Peace and Pain

The day started peacefully enough. English muffins and orange juice on the patio. No movement except a flutter of leaves now and then and a cardinal munching its breakfast at the bird feeder. In my Bible I read about peace—peace for my children. I underlined the verse and marked it: Promise for today: "All your sons will be taught by the Lord, and great will be your children's peace . . . and you will have nothing to fear" (Isa. 54:13–14).

"Come quick! Nicky's hurt." The words of my son's friend Scotty tumbled out in a frightened little wail. "There's blood gushing from his foot."

I'd watched Nicky and friends disappear down the street ten minutes before. They were running in the grass alongside a fire truck that was checking fire hydrants.

"Lord, keep us all calm," I prayed as I raced toward the scene. An assortment of firemen and children huddled around Nicky. A police car pulled in behind the big red fire truck. Down the hill came the paramedic truck, lights flashing, siren wailing.

"Deep laceration," the paramedic said as he cleaned the wound and applied pressure to stop the bleeding. "E.R. should handle it just fine. You want us to run him in or do you want to take him?"

Nicky's face looked white against the green grass. "I'll take him," I said, trying to sound calm.

When it was just the two of us on our way to the hospital Nicky spoke. He'd been brave; now he could cry. "Mommy," his voice quivered. "Mommy. My all-star game. It's day after tomorrow. Will I be OK by then?"

We both knew he wouldn't. I saw the pain in his blue eyes—not a deep kind of pain, but the kind that comes when your heart has held a dream for a long time and suddenly it is snatched away. His tears came unchecked.

"Nicky, I'm sorry." I took his little hand in mine. "You know Nicky, sometimes God teaches us the most through our disappointments. But it still hurts, doesn't it?"

Later that week, with his bandaged foot propped up in front of him, Nicky watched the Little League all-star game from the sidelines. He was trying hard to be brave, but I knew the pain he felt. It hurt to see him suffer.

Then I recalled the promise I'd read in Isaiah: "Your sons shall be taught by the Lord, and great will be your children's peace." I reviewed what I already understood—that God sometimes takes my children through pain in order to teach them about peace. It was up to me to simply trust God's style of instruction for Nicky.

Nicky's foot healed quickly. Only a small scar lingers as a silent reminder of God's lesson.

About Your Timing, Lord . . .

My doctor's words over the phone left me stunned. "Ruth, the mammogram has revealed a suspicious mass in your left breast. I want you to see a surgeon."

Standing there in the middle of my kitchen that cold November day I suddenly felt alone, forsaken. *God, did You forget? I'm the one who is just getting over a car accident. Remember? I was hit by that utility truck three weeks ago tomorrow. About Your timing, Lord . . .*

I struggled to replay the doctor's phone conversation to Mark, but the words got hung up on my emotions.

"I'm not sure I could ever face anything like that," I'd always said when anyone had talked about breast cancer experiences to me. Two of my aunts had died of that dread disease, so such stories always hit much too close to home. Now that the storyline *had* come home, my mind was desperately trying to decide what to do with it.

Suddenly, it was as though I were watching a performance on a screen, except *I* was in the picture. I saw myself responding to Mark's strong arms of comfort, steadying my voice, wiping my eyes, taking a deep breath.

"God will give us courage to face whatever we have to face," I said. "Right now it's time to take the children to school. Please don't worry. I'll be all right. I'll call the surgeon this morning."

I could tell he didn't want to leave, but his classes were waiting. I waved him out the door.

Two weeks later I lay in my hospital bed watching the flurry of activity around me. Another hour and the surgeon would begin his exploration, removing the mass and carefully searching for life-or-death cells.

"Just a little something to help you relax." The nurse took the syringe from the tray she carried. The needle did its work.

Fifteen minutes later she returned. "Ruth, are you asleep already? That shot worked fast on you. Probably because you've been so relaxed all along." She gently lifted my arm and took my pulse. I knew she was talking about resources I didn't have on my own.

Later, after the test results came back marked benign, I thought back to that cold November day when the doctor first called and to the morning of surgery when the countdown was at one hour. I recalled how miraculously and silently God's peace changed from something I talked about to something I knew for a fact. Sometimes there is no other way to learn.

Listen to the pain of your life.
What do you hear?

PART II: WHEN I AM SILENT . . . GOD SPEAKS

CHAPTER FOUR

Interruptions

Please Interrupt

Sometimes I feel like an interruption,
and then I want to shrink
back into my shell
and never come out again.
I want to walk away and say,
"I'm sorry I took your time."

Being an interruption hurts.
It tells me
something is more important than I am.
It tells me
to hurry up and move along.
It tells me
you are looking
but don't see me.
It tells me
you are listening

but don't hear me.
And so I move along.

But, God says,
"Don't hurry away.
Stick around.
Tell me how it is with you.
Tell me what you're feeling
right this minute.
Tell me why you feel that way.
I want to know you.
You count with me.
I care about you.
Tell me what I can do for you."

And I go away feeling
He was glad I called.

Stranger in My House

I sat up in bed. I wasn't dreaming; there *were* voices coming from my kitchen. What was going on at 12:30 in the morning? I didn't have to wonder long. Mark came into the bedroom to reassure me.

"It's Tom," he explained in a whisper. "He's been drinking again. This time the police nabbed him for driving while under the influence. He has nowhere else to go. Some good hot coffee will sober him up. Then I'll put him to bed on the family room couch."

I stared at my pastor-husband through the 12:30 A.M. haze. "He's drunk, and you brought him *here?*" I didn't even know the man—except that he was somebody's uncle and Mark was trying to help him. My mind immediately shifted into high gear.

You can never tell with strangers—especially when they've been drinking. I've heard stories on the news about people who trusted strangers and were murdered or brutally assaulted. You can't trust people you don't know. What about the kids? What if they get hurt? And what about our valuables?

After Mark returned to the kitchen, I watched the glowing green hands of my alarm clock crawl through the early morning hours and waited for the inevitable outburst of violence. None came. I smelled coffee and heard Mark's calm voice.

Finally the house was quiet. Mark came to bed, but for me sleep did not come. I felt the presence of the stranger in my house. I had entertained guests many times. I prided myself on always having my coffeepot plugged in and my favorite brand of muffins stockpiled in the freezer for unexpected drop-ins.

Tonight we had had an unexpected drop-in. Why was he so hard to accept? Were my blueberry muffins and Columbian coffee only to be served to *my* kind of people? Did my front porch doormat say "Welcome" only to those I knew and loved? Could only "safe" people sit and rest in my walnut rocker?

From somewhere in the back of my mind came Christ's penetrating questions of Matthew 5:46–47 NASB: "For if you love those who love you, what reward have you? . . . And if you greet your brothers only, what do you do more than others?"

I concluded that my Christianity isn't very credible if my coffeepot is always hot for friends who drop by, but my house is cold to strangers. Christianity is unique because it causes us to bring out our best coffee and blueberry muffins and offer them to strangers in need. Christianity is unique because it silently yet powerfully urges us to forget ourselves and think of others—even when it happens to be someone's uncle who has had too much to drink.

The Wasteland

"It's hard to withstand an enemy when you don't know . . . who he is or how he operates. Unexpected enemies are our greatest foes." The United States General looked tired and worn. Three agonizing weeks ago a member of the overseas diplomatic corps had disappeared. While walking from his home toward the American Embassy, with American soldiers practicing drills at a nearby base, he was snatched into oblivion.

The General spoke of political and military maneuvers, but he could just as well have been speaking of spiritual operations, the similarities were so obvious. Ignorance of the opposition always leaves room for surprise attacks. And surprise attacks often end in defeat.

One distinguishing fact about spiritual conflict is that it is usually most intense just after victory. It happened that way with Jesus. He had just received the Holy Spirit,

God's stamp of approval, signifying that He was qualified for His assignment. Then came the wilderness—the harsh, barren wasteland west of the Jordan Valley. For the Son of God, the wasteland followed the victory celebration.

I have seen similar patterns in my own life and remember one instance in particular. For three days I had given my all during a retreat for pastors' wives. The women had been warm and generous. They applauded my stories about how I was learning to share my husband when others needed him, and complimented my three-point outlines on gracious giving and flexibility.

"It's where you've lived," they said when it was all over. "We can tell." I flew home in the clouds, aware of God's enablement.

I was still in the clouds the next day when our family set out for homecoming festivities at a nearby college. The happiest thing about the day was that we were all together.

Together, that is, until one of our parishioners spotted my husband as we headed for the football field. "Oh, Mark, Grace needs you right away! Please go to her. She's terribly frightened."

Immediately I felt the wasteland. The sun was scorching and the mountaintops were far away. I walked alone with the children toward the game. *Hadn't I shared Mark enough? Couldn't we have just one day together this week?* My giving was no longer gracious. My "flexibility" had turned to steel, my day to gray.

As we squeezed into a bleacher full of bodies, I suddenly realized that this was where my tidy three-point outlines would either stand or fall. God's test for me was not to be on the mountaintop but in the wilderness.

Then it hit me: The enemy is smart enough to know that my lofty times are also my most vulnerable. Next time I won't be so surprised at his silent, subtle strategy.

Sermon in an Airport

O'Hare airport can be a fun place when everything is on schedule. But on a Friday night in the middle of a blinding, Midwest blizzard, when flights are being delayed, re-routed, and canceled, it can be like a bad dream come true, especially with two impatient children who are anxious for Daddy to come home.

I had exhausted my supply of things to do with my nine- and five-year-old: We had played hide-and-seek through rows of semi-enclosed telephone booths, follow-the-leader up and down the escalators, and hopscotch on the square tiles at the end of Concourse C.

Time crawled through the two-and-a-half hours. Nothing changed on the arrival monitors. The crowds were restless. So were we. Thoughts turned toward home—a hot dinner and a warm bed.

I left home expecting a quick pickup at the airport and

nothing more, but the blizzard had caught up with us. There was a storm between the airport and home, a flight from Denver somewhere overhead, two hungry, tired children by my side, and $2.04 in my purse. We had just enough money to get us out of the parking garage, yet I knew we needed food.

"I'll have two scoops of chocolate ice cream, please, and three glasses of water," I half whispered to the waitress in the coffee shop. I'd figured carefully. With tax, the bill would come to $1.78.

"But, Mommy, we'll have to spend the night in the parking garage." Nine-year-old Jori's face showed signs of panic. "We don't have enough money to get out!"

"Let's wait and see," I whispered, trying to use my most confident, cheerful voice. "Eat your ice cream," I said as visions of an all-night airport camp-out filled my mind.

Finally I motioned to the waitress for our bill.

"You're taken care of," she said, smiling as though she were in on a secret. "The couple over there picked up your tab when they left."

I felt as if someone had just given me a warm hug on a cold night. *Who were those people disappearing from my view? And why did they do this for us?* All I had noticed about them was that one had been wearing a white fur coat. That was all I would ever know about either of them.

I looked at the children across the table. "God says we shouldn't worry about what we're going to eat because He knows even before we do what we will need. I guess when He said it, He really meant it, didn't He?"

Jori and Nicky nodded, their eyes wide with excitement. I knew we would never forget that snowy night and God's silent sermon assuring us of His care and provision.

The Chocolate Monster

The Saturday evening routine was typical for our family—no hint of the extraordinary. I hurried the children through their usual bathing and hair-washing ritual. With one eye on the clock and the other on Winnie-the-Pooh, I performed the story hour obligations. After a quick little "talk to Jesus" for each and a hasty good-night kiss, I turned out their lights and closed their doors. A few last-minute words of instruction to the baby-sitter and we were off. Nothing unusual.

The January evening was typical for Chicago—cold, icy, and snowy—no hint of crisis. Mark drove with extra caution. "Can't be too careful with this ice," he observed. He was right, of course, but I didn't give it much thought. Long ago I had gotten over routine fears. Icy roads didn't bother me. As a matter of fact, there wasn't a lot that really did bother me when it came to fears. I often threw caution to the wind and proceeded at my own pace, which was usually breakneck speed.

I was confident enough not to be bothered by fears, and at times was unsympathetic to those who were. "You can't let your fear paralyze you," I would glibly spout off if someone confided in me. I knew little about fear as I rang the doorbell and joined the party that cold January night.

The warmth and happiness of the evening made the time slip quickly away. The group around me was a happy one, and I felt very much at home in the crowd. They were my people. They were the ones with whom I had laughed and cried my way through college. I was relaxed. I was contented. As I rambled back over the past ten years, I appreciated more than ever God's good gifts to me.

Many of us hadn't seen each other since college, so the dinner party chatter included reminisces about every major and minor event of our lives for the ten years since we had all been together. Everyone was talking at once. We had so much catching up to do. Pictures to pass around, stories about our children to compare, and "remember when" jokes to laugh about. No one could stop talking. But suddenly they did. The chatter stopped. Words were left hanging in midair. And I was trying desperately to hang on to my life.

The interruption came without warning. My words stuck in my throat, halted by a piece of chocolate brownie. I opened my mouth. Nothing came out—not even a cough. I frantically reached for Mark. No words. No breath. Nothing except that frantic grab. The conversation faded. The room dimmed. Nothing . . . except desperate efforts to gasp. But there were no gasps, only a lifetime of seconds. Then strong arms grabbed me around my waist and strong hands pushed inward.

The evening was suddenly silent. My coffee was cold

and the culprit brownie lay half eaten on my plate. The room was so quiet all I could hear was my own breathing. Everyone else seemed to be listening for that sound too. It was there, but it was weak and tired. The party ended. Gentle hands helped me to the car and home.

The physical trauma of those breathless moments wore off after a night of deep, uninterrupted sleep. But the emotional trauma did not. I sat down to eat the breakfast Mark prepared for me. I could not eat. My throat tightened. My head started to spin. I could feel my heart pounding. I had to excuse myself from the table.

I continued to be plagued with a paralyzing fear. What if it happened when no one was around? What if it happened in front of the children? Whenever I thought about Saturday night, I would feel my heart starting to race and my throat starting to tighten. All my neat little theories about mind-over-matter went out the window. I felt fear. It was physical fear. My confident self-control was gone. Fear was controlling me. I was helpless.

The paralysis of fear was as draining for me as were those few breathless seconds. The day of fear extended into two days and then three. Each meal, no matter how tempting, became a battleground of mind over stomach. Each day became an effort to keep my mind from reliving the whole paralyzing scene. A chocolate brownie had become the ruler of my life.

In desperation, I searched my file for the folder stuffed with newspaper clippings about safety and first aid. I found an article I remembered reading a year ago about a hug that had saved many lives from a choking death. Somehow Mark too had remembered the article. I felt those lines of print. As I read, I could feel the familiar pounding of my heart and tightening of my throat.

The article told how to help someone who was

choking. I copied the suggestions on a three-by-five card and taped it to my most conspicuous kitchen cabinet door, right next to the list of emergency phone numbers. Then I stood in front of the bathroom mirror and, with newspaper clipping in front of me, rehearsed exactly what I would do if I choked while I was alone. My fears continued.

In the midst of my agonizing battle, I remembered a promise of liberation from God: "God did not give us a spirit of timidity but a spirit of power and love and self-control" (2 Timothy 1:7 RSV). If this battle were going to be won, I suddenly realized, God needed my cooperation. I described my fears to God just as I had to Mark.

And then I ate brownies. I purposely went out and bought the nuttiest chocolate brownies I could find. I ate four at one time. Each swallow was traumatic. My heart still pounded and my stomach violently rebelled against the chocolate offering. But I ate the brownies.

My excuses at mealtime stopped. I glued myself to my chair until I had eaten every bite. Before each meal, my silent conversation to God became, "God, You have not given me this spirit of fear, so it must be my own doing. You have given me power and self-control. Therefore, I will eat this meal in peace."

And I did. Before the week was over, Saturday night was a vague memory that evoked little emotion. I remembered the dinner. I remembered the noisy conversations and the happy reminiscing. I even remembered how good the chocolate brownies had tasted. Now, many months removed from that January night, I remember the monster of fear that held me in its grip, and I thank the Lord for the freedom to eat chocolate brownies and to truly enjoy them. It was as though in those few terrifying moments of silence I had lived a lifetime. Never again would I take so lightly the agonizing reality of fear.

The Cardboard Window

The thick gray smog that hung overhead matched the gray mood I felt as we drove through Chicago's west side ghetto. Even though the calendar said spring, the day was bleak and cold. The remainders of a recent snow storm lay in black, ugly heaps along curbs and streets. Trickles from melting black snow moved bits of debris and litter toward street gutters. Slush and dirt were everywhere. I unconsciously pulled my white spring coat closer, as though to keep the city from touching me.

People too were everywhere. Small, innocent faces appeared beside newspaper shacks on street corners. "Newspapers," they called weakly with equally small voices. Boys with clothes many sizes too big leaped over fire hydrants and scooted down narrow muddy alleys in search of excitement. A gang of girls with black leather jackets stood in a huddle along a curb and glared at us when we stopped at a red light. Men with empty faces leaned against dimly lit barber shops and cluttered laundromats. Mothers coming home from work got off buses and stopped at the corner grocery store to buy food for the evening meal.

We had just entered the land of the Latin Counts. Signs and symbols scrawled on the sides of buildings proclaimed their domain. A gang meeting was being held in front of one deserted garage. A few inattentive members played hockey in the street. As we slowed to avoid their game, I reached across and locked the door on my side of the car.

I shifted my eyes from the people. School buildings with broken windows and barred doors, tiny concrete playgrounds, dingy store-front churches, row after row of apartment houses with sagging wooden stairs and cardboard in place of window panes—all blurred together for me. I suddenly felt very tired and weary.

At last we saw our destination, a tiny store-front mission. It was almost dark, and the light from the third-floor apartment of our friends beckoned a warm welcome. We securely locked our car, and I tightened my hold on my purse as we tried to avoid puddles of melting snow and sidewalk debris. Past the delicatessen, up three flights of stairs, and through the open door of the home of our host and hostess for the evening. I relaxed as the door closed behind us.

The evening passed quickly and pleasantly. All was warm and secure and comfortable. We were three flights above it all.

As the clock struck ten, my thoughts turned toward home—home with its wide, tree-lined streets, landscaped lawns, and neat, well-kept homes. At home I could walk down the street and relax. At home I felt safe and secure.

Some families in our neighborhood were poorer than ours, some very poor, but the teenagers did not haunt the streets in tight-lipped groups, and the city street department kept streets and sidewalks clean.

At home were no broken windows or cardboard replacements, no boarded up store fronts or barred doors. At home, mothers went to the supermarket in taxicabs or in the family's second car. On the Northwestern express train, well-dressed fathers returned from a day of business in the Loop, careful to leave their boots and the city's dirt outside. At home there were swimming pools, tennis courts, and golf courses. At home there were million-dollar churches and clean, modern schools with football fields, stadiums, and fieldhouses. Yes, it was time to go home.

I kept my eyes closed most of the way home—perhaps because I was tired, perhaps because I wanted to forget, perhaps because I didn't want to be reminded of the difference. I was especially glad to be going home. I opened my eyes as the car slowed down and we turned the last corner. I loved the evergreen trees that framed our little home. They looked almost enchanted with a light layer of snow covering their branches. On the window ledge of our large living room window I could see my prized collection of crystal goblets that I had collected on our travels. The antique lamp above the kitchen table glowed a warm welcome as we pulled in the driveway beside our second car. Yes, it was good to be home.

The crunch of glass under my feet as I stepped through the door told me something was wrong. My heart sank as I looked around the kitchen. Shattered glass was everywhere. The curtains at the front window billowed freely in the night air. Pieces of white sink enamel lay scattered amid the glass. On the counter next to the sink lay a large, jagged rock. A gust of cold air snapped the torn curtains, giving me a brief glimpse down the street. In that silent moment I saw a long, long way. And when I looked at the piece of cardboard that replaced our shattered window the next morning, I saw even further. God's peace can walk the city streets, and sometimes violence comes to the suburbs. It took a cardboard window pane to help me learn.

Listen to the interruptions in your life.
What do you hear?

CHAPTER FIVE

Independence

A Man Went Free

A man went free the day You died.
Barabbas.
Hero.
Macho Man.
The People's Choice.
They cut his chains and
buried his past
in his empty prison cell.
Murder. Insurrection.
It didn't matter.

But they nailed You down,
Strapped You with the weight of a cross,
While he walked away clean.
They restored his dignity to him:
Free man.
Pardoned.
No more labels.
But they stripped You,
Gave You thorns for Your crown.

A weed for Your scepter
And an obituary that read:
JESUS, KING OF THE JEWS.

They shouted his name through the city.
Blazed it in neon lights
and put a marquee around it
While they drove You to the place
of the Skull,
Gave You vinegar to drink,
and threw dice for Your clothing.
When darkness came,
You bowed Your head
and died
alone
While he celebrated in the streets
with the Passover crowd.

A man went free the day You died.
I was that man.

Struggle Under the Sink

The noise under the kitchen sink was horrendous. Most of the commotion was mechanical, but some of it was human—my own grunts and groans—as I wrestled with the wrench I thought would unjam the garbage disposal.

Mark *had* to have heard! He wasn't deaf. Most of the clatter I was making was for his benefit. But there he sat, upstairs at his desk preparing his class lecture, totally oblivious to my struggles under the sink.

After several intense but unsuccessful attempts to play plumber, I was convinced my pounding head would be forever tilted at a ninety-degree angle. The red, angry imprint of the wrench branded the palm of my hand. Admitting defeat, I finally swallowed my pride, held my aching head, and called for Mark.

"I have been working on this stubborn garbage disposal half the morning. My head hurts and my hand will never be the same. Would you *please* see what you can do?"

"Why didn't you call me sooner?" he asked. "There's a little red button at the back that you have to reset before it will work."

This time I knew he heard my groan. His response was a gentle rebuke. "I'm sorry, Honey, but I can't read your mind. I didn't know you needed help. I didn't even hear you down here. Next time, ask me before you get yourself all bent out of shape. Here, let me show you where the button is."

I thought a lot about our garbage disposal episode that day, and I came to the conclusion that many of the breakdowns in marriages probably come because husbands and wives fail to make their needs known to one another. We expect that our loving, sensitive, insightful partners will automatically anticipate our needs, read our thoughts, and accurately interpret all our nonverbal clues.

"Ask and it will be given to you. . . . For everyone who asks receives. . . ." Jesus said one day to his followers (Matt. 7:7–8). Jesus not only *talked* about communicating needs. He *did* it. He asked for a boat when He needed the privacy of the other side of the lake. He asked for a colt when He needed transportation into Jerusalem. He requested the presence of His three closest friends when He faced the grief of Gethsemane.

Scripture teaches need-stating. It's called prayer. If the infinite God of the universe, who knows all my thoughts, wants me to make my requests known to Him, how much more should I be willing to state my needs to my finite husband—to whom the capacity of mind reading has not been given!

Learning Life's Lessons

"Mom, I need new shoes," Nicky announced as he burst through the door after school. "Miss Bell says it's dangerous to run in gym with my toe sticking out."

I looked down at my son's blue tennies. Hadn't I just bought them last month? But the protruding toe, a slit along the side, and tattered laces told me he'd had them longer. "You're right, Nicky. It's time for some new tennies, but you'll have to wait until our next paycheck."

To a seven-year-old, two weeks is an eternity. "But I may break my toe by then," he pleaded. "I need them *now*."

"Sometimes life's lessons are hard to learn, Nicky. Seldom do we get what we want the minute we want it. Here is a chance for you to learn to get along with what you have until we have the money."

"But, Mother," Nicky protested, "I can't wear these shoes for gym anymore. Miss Bell said!"

I launched into an elaborate discourse on budgeting principles. "So you see, Nicky," I concluded, "that's how Mommy and Daddy spend money. Tennis shoes are not in the budget this time; next time they will be."

"Then I'll pray about my shoes," Nicky announced. "I'll tell God I need the money by tomorrow."

My mind did a panic-alert. How could I tell my son that God is not a giant mail-order catalog in the sky? How could I temper his impetuous request with "Thy will be done," when he had already decided what was to be done?

I swallowed hard. "OK, Nicky. Why don't you tell God about your need." Later, when he learned for himself that God does not issue cash on demand, I would explain to him about prayer.

When he left for school the next morning, new tennis shoes were still uppermost on his mind. "Can we buy my shoes tonight? You'll get the money today, because I prayed about it."

"We'll see, Nicky," I replied as I kissed him good-bye. There wasn't time to explain just then.

But the need to explain didn't come; Nicky's answer came instead. "This is long overdue . . . sorry for the oversight," said the note I received in the mail that afternoon. The enclosed check, payment for an article I'd written long ago and forgotten, was more than enough to pay for Nicky's new shoes.

After school, Nicky's blue eyes danced. "See, Mom I told you it would come. Now can we buy my shoes?"

Today Nicky wears new blue-and-gold tennis shoes—poignant reminders of a child's simple trust and of my need to continually relearn what faith is all about.

When the Ropes Come Down

Ropes in a swimming pool can be a nuisance. The bright yellow bobbers strung along the ropes look festive—like Japanese lanterns at an evening patio picnic—but who needs Japanese lanterns while swimming? They take up valuable space. Three bobbers in a row equals the width of one body. Someone always has to wait in the whirlpool because bobbers instead of people are floating in the lanes.

My suggestion? Keep the ropes out of the pool so more people can swim free and relaxed and without the fear of strangling themselves on a two-inch nylon cord. No boundaries. No worries about crossing over into someone else's lane. The whole pool is my lane.

One day our aquatics director got smart and took down the ropes for the early bird swim. Suddenly the pool was twice as wide, the bodies twice as many. Creative water works. We could swim free style. Chart our own course. Navigate circles, diagonals, diamonds, cubicles, if we wanted. Straight lines got old quickly. For thirty minutes I swam "free."

But in those thirty minutes, I was clobbered on the head by what felt like a two-hundred-pound butterfly stroke, gouged by a frog kick that violated my space, and asked politely if I would please swim next to the wall because I kept crossing into the next lane.

I climbed out of the pool feeling tense and irritable. The nerve of that woman to say I crossed her lane when there weren't even any lanes to cross. My head was still thumping from the muscular butterfly flap. Usually I went home from a swim feeling every muscle in my body had been massaged by the gentle waters. Today I was tied in knots, and my swimming skills had definitely deteriorated. My time was way up, my strokes uneven, and my breathing irregular.

Today our aquatics director was even smarter. He put the ropes back up. The 6 A.M. swim was surprisingly more pleasant for everyone. I still would prefer smaller yellow bobbers, but the boundaries? God knows how much better life works when we learn to live within them. I wonder why it takes me so long to learn.

Flying Solo

Overhead a flock of Canada geese spread across the October sky with the order and precision of a squadron of planes flying in formation. As I watched the V-shaped phenomenon honking its way southward, I was reminded of dependency. These nine-pound Canada geese—each measuring three feet in length and cruising thousands of feet in the air at speeds up to sixty miles per hour—may seem to be on their own. But their migratory feats do not depend on individual prowess.

Their secret of long-distance endurance flight is found in their ability to fly in *formation.* Directly behind one bird and in front of the other, each rides the powerful updraft created by its predecessor, depending on another for protection from battering headwinds. Flying solo is not God's plan for Canada geese flying south.

Neither is "flying solo" God's plan for the Christian,

though we sometimes act as if it is. We've been taught to be resilient, independent, strong. Rugged individualism is the "American way." To show that I need another is to show weakness. To lean on someone else means I am deficient. To allow another person to help means I am incapable of helping myself.

So I often fly solo. I try to "tough it out." And too often, ignoring my need for fellow Christians, I fly headlong into battering headwinds.

Evidently the Christians in Corinth had the same tendency because Paul felt it was necessary to write to them concerning their need for one another. According to Paul, we are one body, but many parts. Comparing individuals to parts of the body, he says, "And the eye cannot say to the hand, 'I have no need of you'; or again the head to the feet, 'I have no need of you'" (1 Cor. 12:21 NASB). The parts *need* each other.

What does it mean to need one another? If I need you, I will lay aside my "superwoman" image and let you know that I sometimes feel lonely, that at times I need a call from a friend—someone who knows and loves me and can be a "mirror" to silently reflect my inconsistencies.

Needing another means I won't have to do *all* the serving. It means that when my car breaks down I will allow you to lend me yours. When insecurities hit I will ask you to pray for me. When I feel overwhelmed I will allow you to offer me advice.

Who am I to think I don't need you? Watching that flock of Canada geese fly overhead reminds me that I do!

Listen to the independence in your life.
What do you hear?

CHAPTER SIX

Unearned Love

Splintered Wood

What is this cross I have to bear,
This splintered wood
That rubs against my flesh
Like a strip of coarse sandpaper?
This cross—
This dull, dead weight
That bends my spirits,
Pins hope to the ground?

I stumble along cobbled streets
On my way to my own Golgotha—
The "place of a skull."
I've walked these streets before;
When children skipped,
And old men sang
And young men
Watched the skies with hope.

But shadows fell across those skies.
Now old men mourn.
The children cry.
And the splintered wood
leans heavy on my back.
Darkness drops
Into the middle of the day.
The earth vibrates.
The ground shakes.
It's never been this way before.
Nature's flow erupts like a geyser.
And all around is turmoil.

I reach the city gate.
It is cold outside.
What is this hill I have to climb—
This place of barren rock
and dead-men's bones?
I clutch my cross
and stagger upward in the dark.
There is no other way around.
The wood tears deep into my skin.
Does no one understand my load?
Does no one know
the agony of lonely hills?

But on the stony skull ahead
I see another cross;
Rising out of the shadows,
Silhouetted against the dark.
"This hill," He said,
"Is one that you must climb.
This darkness you must feel.
But your cross—
the one that straps you
with its weight,
I carried once,
Up this same hill
For you
So that today, My child,
you may lay it down
And be free."

A Father's Gift

The storm clouds were gathering inside the car as well as out. Large, wet drops splashed against our windshield as we left church and started for home.

The outer turbulence, however, was easier to cope with than the inner. Our seven-year-old wore the storm on her face, flashed it in her eyes. Absolutely nothing was right in the back seat. Nicky had his foot over the middle hump, much too close to her semi-new sandals. The breeze from Mom's window was too cold, and the way Daddy dodged the road repairs was giving her a stomach ache.

There was nothing very positive to be said about her actions either. She smacked her gum, snapped at her brother, and sucked in her breath for special effect every time her daddy hit a bump in the road. All in all, the tempest in the back seat was something I chose not to tolerate. I opened my mouth to pronounce judgment, but Mark was there first.

"Jori. Nothing is going right for you today, is it? You are usually so positive. I want you to know that I love you." He slowed the car, turned around and smiled at her, choosing at that moment to not dwell on her actions but to affirm her character.

Her defenses crumbled. The storm subsided. The rest of the ride was peaceful. Spoken words of love and praise had overcome the turmoil.

In the Old Testament, the father, as God's representative of the home, conferred blessings upon his children. While the word "bless" in Scripture often means "to declare happy," the same Hebrew word "barak" and the Greek "eulogeo," may also be translated "to speak well of" or "to praise." We don't generally think of stormy rides home from church as a time to bless (praise or speak well of) our children, but I'm convinced that on that day, Mark gave Jori a gift she will use for years to come. By praising her, he taught her to praise others.

"If there be any praise," Paul says in Philippians 4:8 (KJV), "think [dwell] on these things." What better place to start dwelling on praise than with our children—even in the midst of storms.

Under No Conditions

"I love you," I said to a spotless face. No blueberry jam. No milk mustache. Each strand of hair in its proper place. "I've signed your report card. It's lying on the counter so you won't forget it. I'm proud of all those A's. Mrs. Harmon should be proud too."

I gave him an extra hug before he raced out and hopped on his red ten-speed. It glistened as much as his face that morning. "Your bike looks so clean. You must have worked hard to make it shine so much."

He waved good-bye, his new blue jacket billowing behind him. He looked handsome. The gray in his plaid shirt perfectly highlighted the blue-gray of his twinkling eyes. He had even chosen the right pants. Gray cords with a blue and gray striped belt.

"Yes, I do love that little guy," I said to myself as I turned to the morning clutter. Even his blue cereal bowl and plate were rinsed and stacked neatly in the dishwasher. So easy to love him when he's doing things right.

That was yesterday. Today he wants to help me in the kitchen. He has on dirty football pants, the ones with a big rip in the knee, and the old yellow football jersey that I had hid in his bottom drawer. It has stretched so much it is several sizes too big, and besides, yellow makes him look jaundiced.

He volunteers to help unload the groceries. As he climbs onto the countertop—football pants and all—the flour falls off the shelf, shattering my glass coffeepot in a thousand pieces. The can of frozen orange juice, intended for the freezer, misses its mark and hits my foot instead.

"Sorry, Mom. Didn't mean to do it."

I massage my little toe. "It hurts just as bad either way, you know." He doesn't seem to know.

Dinner is next on the agenda. My volunteer hangs around, and I put him in charge of the spaghetti. The water begins to boil, but the noodles slide out of the wrong end of the box as he carries it to the stove. He heads for the broom again.

"Out. Please. Out of the kitchen." His shoulders slump as he walks out the back door.

Then I think of the One who loves me when my face is dirty, hugs me when I've broken more than coffeepots, keeps His arms around me even when I've caused Him pain.

I go to the picnic table where Nicky sits with his head down. I encircle him in my arms.

"Honey, I love you." That was all I needed to say. His arms went around me and his dirty cheek rested against mine.

"Lord, keep me giving him hugs, especially when I think he least deserves them. Because that's what you do for me."

Rocks Don't Cry

Fathers don't cry.
They are
  Brave and strong,
  Steadfast and sure,
  Like a rock that never moves.
No time for tears,
Too controlled to cry.
Their world is concrete and asphalt,
Logic and logistics.
Rocks don't cry.
Neither do dads.

But you cried that day, Dad.
You wept for my rebelliousness.
Like the Father over Jerusalem,
You waited on the front porch for me,
Long after the lights were off.
You waited and wondered
While I
  Made my own choices,
  Ignored the fences,

And then came home hoping you didn't know.
But you did.
Your tears washed over my rebellion,
Softened my will.
And I knew I was loved.

Rocks don't cry.
Neither do dads.
But you did that day.
You wept over my pain.
Like the man from Galilee who cried
at His friend's grave,
You watched
as the blood squirted from my vein,
Threatening a pipeline to life.
You held my hand
as the doctor sutured the skin
ripped by a fall on broken glass.
You felt my groans.
And afterward I saw your tears,
Trickles of tenderness.
Your tears washed over my hurt,
And I knew I was loved.

Rocks don't cry.
Neither do dads.
But you cried that day.
You wept over separation.
Like the One who cried in the garden,
You wiped your eyes with your big white handkerchief
Unashamedly
In front of all my friends
As the big white ocean liner
Pulled away from the dock
For seven days and 3,000 miles of
Atlantic Ocean.
You were the only dad who came;
Rode the Greyhound bus for 12 hours
just to wave good-bye
And cry.
Your tears washed over the miles between us.

UNEARNED LOVE

Your big white handkerchief
Brought us together,
Held us together,
And I knew I was loved.
For in those tears
I saw strength.
My rock,
My Dad,
Who knew how to cry.

Listen to the unearned love in your life.
What do you hear?

CHAPTER SEVEN

Gains and Losses

Of Kingdoms and Crosses

I love you John, Peter, James, Andrew.
Here, let me offer you a kingdom.
First-vice president
Joint chief of staff
Right-hand man.
See that door?
We'll write our name in gold upon it.
See that mountain?
We'll build our tabernacle in the clouds.
One for you
One for me
And one for Elijah.
See those crowds?
We'll autograph our books
Sign them up for seminars
Put them on our mailing list.
I love you John.
Here's your three-piece-double-breasted suit
Your credit card
And your personal copy of
How to Win Friends and Influence People.

I love you Peter.
Here, let me teach you how to preach.
Three points.
Illustrations.
And a closing line for the cameras.

I love you James.
Church salesman of the year.
Your territory is everything west of the Jordan.
Direct mail will do.
Here's your ad copy writer.

I love you Andrew.
Let me multiply your loaves and fishes.
Contests.
Concerts.
Creative worship.
Keep those buses rolling in.

But
He went to a cross and died.
Strange way to build a kingdom.
Strange way to say I love you.

Lost and Found

"Being lost is when you're meant to be somewhere you're not." My nine-year old's answer was so simple it was profound. I could tell he knew whereof he spoke. His drama had started several hours earlier—just about dusk.

"Where's Nick?" Mark asked as he pulled the Datsun into the garage and prepared to close the doors for the night.

"I haven't seen him for hours. I thought he was with you." My words sounded the alarm in my brain. I could read concern in Mark's usually calm voice. "He and Jerry rode up to the park about three. I told him to be home by four."

I phoned the neighborhood circuit. Nicky was in none of his usual spots. Jerry had come home at four, almost two hours earlier. The last he knew, Nick was riding his bike on the dirt mounds out behind the library—the ones closest to the reservoir.

Suddenly everything was out of sync. Terrifying visions formed in my mind as we jumped in the car and headed toward the reservoir.

Even the twilight, usually gentle for me, seemed sinister and threatening. Nick was somewhere out in those shadows. And he was the kind of guy who always came home.

The night cadences had already begun to rise from the creekbed that bordered the library. Mark chose the creek path and I turned west toward the reservoir.

"N-i-c-k-y . . ." my call bounced between the mounds of dirt.

By day the hills were a constant source of adventure for nine-year-old dirt-bike enthusiasts, but this evening they loomed like monsters, and the reservoir beyond yawned hungrily.

Where was he? I felt the empty wilderness around me and shivered in its silence.

Suddenly, out from a clump of dried grasses and cattails, a small voice said, "Here I am, Mom. I'm on my way home."

The mud-figure, adorned in a wet and soggy baseball shirt that stretched out from under a dirt-plastered jacket, moved slowly toward me. Nicky carried his musket—a $7.95 replica of those used in Revolutionary War days, a souvenir from Williamsburg, Virginia. A powderhorn he had made himself was slung across his shoulders.

"Trey and I were fighting the Redcoats . . . except I forgot what time it was."

My tears finished the story for him. In fact, the three of us huddled there in a cold little clump and cried tears of relief. It was the only punishment Nicky needed.

"Mom, I'm really sorry," he said later that night as he snuggled beside me for his bedtime story. "I like it better when I'm home with you and Dad."

I thought of the One who grieves over my wanderings; who pursues me when I am meant to be somewhere I am not. There is no peace in being lost, because I was created to be found.

"The Good Life"

Bankrupt! The word has a sinister ring. It was what happened to someone else's family business, never to yours. But this time "bankrupt" seemed to be plastered all over the walls that for four generations had held our family enterprise together.

"The plant is closed," my dad said over the phone. "Boarded up and barred. The bank owns it now."

His voice sounded tired. What does a sixty-two-year-old man say when his life's blood has just been clamped off?

A million thoughts jostled around in my mind. I had wanted so much more for my parents in their retirement years—more than frozen assets, a lost inheritance, and a boarded-up industrial complex.

Hadn't they lived through enough financial headaches? Sacrificed more than enough to put their five children through school? Experienced more than their share of lean years? Why couldn't they enjoy a taste of "the good life?" If two people ever deserved it, my folks did.

I had wanted them to retire in comfort. Nothing extravagant. Just enough security to enjoy some extras that life had never afforded them—a trip to Ecuador to visit a missionary friend, Sunday dinners out, a new carpet for their upstairs bedroom.

This whole thing is like a car rolling downhill backward, I thought last week when we visited Mother and Dad. *Here they are, working harder than ever with less to show for it. Odds and ends of house-painting jobs. Long, hot hours and a few commission sales for a local monument company. Do-it-yourself projects. Canning and freezing to cut the cost of groceries.*

I wished I could reverse the trend, pay to have their leaky faucets fixed, buy them a new mattress, a new carpet for their upstairs bedroom, a year's supply of steaks.

"The only treasure you take to heaven with you is your children," Dad said one night as he looked proudly around the table at his children and grandchildren. He prayed with us, then left to visit a man who had lost an arm, three fingers, and both eyes in a dynamite accident. It was time for their weekly Bible study.

As I watched Dad disappear into the silent evening, I remembered what Jesus said on the subject: "Lay not up for yourselves treasures upon earth . . . but lay up . . . treasures in heaven" (Matt. 6:19-20 KJV). Then it dawned on me that my folks *were* enjoying the good life. Giving them a new carpet for their bedroom suddenly didn't seem so important after all—not when compared to their lifetime of contented service to others.

Blooms in the Desert

Nothing about her appearance indicated success. For thirty years she had lived alone in two tiny rooms of adobe brick in a remote Indian village. Working tirelessly in a dispensary that opened its doors around the clock to pain, sickness, and suffering, my missionary friend had had no time to pamper herself.

We sat on the bare concrete of her front porch, sucked on ice cubes that had cooled our lemonade, and munched peanut butter crackers. One hundred-and-two degree heat steamed from the sun-baked earth, melted the ice in our glasses, and rolled down our faces in trickles of perspiration. Her life's companion, a mangy, long-haired mutt, thumped his tail now and then against the shadow of the pinon pine. Nothing else moved. Civilization had wound down.

I looked across the field of yucca and sage to the

church. No steeple, only a squatty square of red clay topped by layers of thatch that came to a point in the middle.

We had gone last night into that clay cathedral to sing and pray. Evening vespers, Marjorie had called it. She'd pumped out "Amazing Grace" on the portable organ as though she were playing a Bach fugue on the 6,000 pipes of St. Paul's in London. Her white tennis shoes never paused on the pedals. Three delicate pink roses, an offering from her tiny, triangular rose garden that grew just outside her kitchen door, graced the rough-hewn altar plank. *Blooms in the desert* I thought as I breathed in the fragrance.

Not many had come to worship under the thatch. A handful of barefoot waifs, who looked as if they had neither washcloth nor mother, sat straight and quiet on the front row of the backless benches, their dark eyes shining, their hands folded reverently in their laps. Several men in straw sandals and white shirts led the service. Their wives sat on the opposite side of the aisle, holding squirming babies and smiling during the entire service. Marjorie moved unobtrusively from organ to front row and when the vespers ended she gave a personal benediction—a warm hug—to everyone present. I couldn't understand her words, but I understood the smiles of pleasure they produced. The barefoot waifs hung on to her skirt and the leaders never took their eyes from her as she spoke. No one had to lock the door as we left because there wasn't one. Marjorie folded up her organ and we carried it down the path toward home.

"Aren't they marvelous people?" she asked later as she mixed powdered milk and water for our bedtime snack. "The men who led tonight were little boys I've watched grow up. Daniel has even been to Bible school." She spoke with the pride of a mother, smiled with the glow of youth. I noticed how free her face was of lines, despite her fifty-some years. She served the powdered milk in crystal goblets and put another dish of peanut butter crackers before us. The evening ritual had the air of high-tea.

This was our final evening. Tomorrow we would begin a two-day trek back to paved roads and concrete bridges. But first we would cross 130 miles of nature's desolation. Marjorie and I sat on the bare cement of her porch, which by now had been cooled by the evening's chill, and looked west toward the Sierra Madres in the distance.

"It's such beautiful country here, we really don't need roses," Marjorie said. "But I plant them just the same." I looked again at the sage and the yucca growing amid swatches of brown. She had said "beautiful." There was no doubt she had meant it.

"No place in all the world has sunsets like this." She spoke with the conviction of one who for many years had been looking over sage brush and yucca and seeing nothing but splendid sunsets over the sierras.

"Contentment is natural wealth; luxury, artificial poverty," the Greek philosopher Socrates once said. I knew there in that silent, isolated hamlet of central Mexico that I had witnessed contentment first hand.

Simplicity Lost

"Joy to the world! The Lord is come."

I looked for joy as I window-shopped with the Christmas crowd at one of our city's most fashionable shopping centers. The store was a decorated menagerie of costly merchandise from all over the world, and the shoppers who dished out fifty- and one-hundred-dollar bills for holiday "trinkets" reflected tastes and styles as international as the merchandise they purchased.

I looked for joy in the Madison Avenue celebration, in the faces of people who could buy two-thousand-dollar jade rings from Shanghai or fifteen-hundred-dollar teakwood trays from Burma.

I looked for joy, but I saw worry lines etched deep across their foreheads. I saw staccato gazes focusing on things, not people. I heard blasts of cold and impatient words. Frantic steps. Push. Shove. Buy. "Joy to the world"?

The scene brought other faces to my mind—contrasting images of another time, another place. A damp, dark street in a littered corner of Mexico City. A *mercado* filled with chunks of hanging pork, crates of live chickens, buckets of beady-eyed fish. Sights and sounds of Christmas? Precious few *centavos* exchanged for an evening meal. Dirt and dark and hunger. The tiny frame of a woman wrapped in a shawl that was sizes too big, calling into the night to advertise the latest edition of the city's *periodico.* A baby asleep behind her on a pile of bundled newsprint.

I shuffled along behind people in a hurry going nowhere. But I smiled into relaxed faces and looked into tranquil eyes. People who saw strangers and took them in. We sometimes communicated without exchanging words.

I sensed simplicity in that dirty back-alley street of Mexico City. Spirits uncomplicated by things, untouched by greed, unaware of artificial needs induced by Madison Avenue propaganda. Contentment. Peace. Joy. In a dirty back-alley street of Mexico City.

At this Christmas season, I'm reminded of a star, a simple stable, a child asleep on a bundle of hay. I wonder how much of that simplicity we have lost in the ribbons, tinsel, and wrappings of Madison Avenue.

"Joy to the world! The Lord is come; let earth receive her King. . . ." Perhaps it's time we get back to the simplicity of Bethlehem—and *there* find our king, our reason for joy.

Contentment Is . . .

I heard the voice but couldn't see the person. She was on the other side of the locker, just coming in from her early morning swim. Her voice sounded like the morning itself—bright, cheerful, and full of life. At 6:15 in the morning, it would catch anyone's attention. I heard its affirming tone.

"Delores, I really appreciated the book you picked up for me last week. I know the library was out of your way. I haven't been able to put the book down. Solzhenitsyn is a great writer. I'm glad you suggested him to me."

"Good morning, Pat," she greeted another swimmer. For a moment the melodious voice was silent, then I heard it again. "Have you ever seen such a gorgeous day? I spied a pair of meadowlarks as I walked over this morning. Makes you glad you're alive, doesn't it?"

The voice was too good to be true. Who can be that

thankful at this time of the morning? Her voice had a note of refinement to it. Probably some rich woman who has nothing to do all day but sip tea on her veranda and read Solzhenitsyn. I suppose I could be cheerful at 6 A.M. if I could swim and read my way through the day. Probably even owns a cottage in the north woods.

I rounded the corner toward the showers and came face to face with the youthful voice. She was just packing her gear. Her yellow housekeeping uniform hung crisp and neat on her fiftyish frame. It was a uniform I'd seen before—along with mops, brooms, dust cloths, and buckets. An employee of the facility at which I swam. She flashed a smile my way, picked up her plastic K-Mart shopping bag, and hurried out the door, spreading "have a glorious day" benedictions as she went.

I still had the yellow uniform on my mind as I swam my laps and sank down among the foamy lather of the whirlpool. My two companions were deep in conversation. At least one of them was. His tired, sad voice told tragic woes of arthritic knees, a heart aneurysm, sleepless nights, and pain-filled days.

Nothing was good or right. The water was too hot, the whirlpool jets weren't strong enough for his stiff knees, and his doctors had been much too slow in diagnosing his case. With his diamond-studded hand, he wiped the white suds out of his face. He looked ancient, but I suspected he too was fiftyish.

The yellow uniform and the diamond studded ring stood out in striking, silent contrast, proof to me again that when God says "Godliness with contentment is great gain," He really means it. This morning I saw both contentment and discontent. I resolved never to forget.

In Comparison

Not every day does a former Miss USA walk into the room and take a seat three people from where I am sitting. The minute I saw her I knew she was no ordinary blue-eyed blonde. The sparkle in her eyes, the grace in her movements, and the confidence in her voice told me she was someone special.

She chatted comfortably with those who knew her and graciously included those of us who didn't. I was glad to be separated from her by three people, for I suddenly felt a striking contrast between Miss USA and me.

Her voice was smooth and mellow. Her perfectly manicured hands lay folded and relaxed on the table's edge. For the first time that evening I had nothing to say. My hands looked rough. My nail polish was chipped. I'd rushed out of the house without taking time to do a repair job. I hadn't noticed my hands before. And when I dressed for the evening, I felt okay about the dusty rose outfit I was wearing. Now, however, in contrast to the vibrant burgundy dress at the other end of the table, mine looked pale and outdated. Until now, the externals hadn't mattered.

By the time my evening with Miss USA was over, I had reduced myself to a second-class citizen. I hadn't traveled the world, spoken to hundreds, or won music scholarships. I had always thought *class* didn't matter. Tonight, I wasn't so sure.

"Ruth!" She reached out and touched my arm as we moved away from the table. Her smile seemed genuine. We stepped back from the group. "I've been wanting to meet you to tell you how God has used your gift to minister to me. Please keep writing for people like me who need it."

My game was over. I knew what I'd been playing. I'd been caught up so much in comparisons that I could not enjoy God's gift in someone else without feeling that it diminished *me*. I went home that evening feeling sad. *The game of comparing,* I thought, *is the root of much unhappiness and dissatisfaction.*

But games don't need to last a lifetime. Sometimes a brief encounter is enough to remind us of God's principles. "Each one should test his own actions. Then he can take pride in himself, without comparing himself to somebody else" (Gal. 6:4). Today that verse is written on an index card and taped above my kitchen sink as a silent reminder that who I am before God is all I have to offer. It is all He wants.

Listen to the gains and losses of your life.
What do you hear?

CHAPTER EIGHT

Tenderness

If I really cared . . .

If I really cared . . .
I would look you in the eyes
when you talk to me;
I would think about what you are saying
rather than what I am going to say next;
I would hear your feelings
as well as your words.

If I really cared . . .
I would listen without defending;
I would hear without deciding
whether you are right or wrong;
I would ask you why,
not just how and when and where.

If I really cared . . .
I would allow you inside of me;
I would tell you my hopes,
my dreams, my fears, my hurts;
I would tell you when I've blown it
and when I've made it.

If I really cared . . .
I would laugh with you but not at you;
I would talk with you and not to you;
And I would know when it is time to do neither.

If I really cared . . .
I wouldn't climb over your walls;
I would hang around until you let me in the gate.
I wouldn't unlock your secrets;
I would wait until you handed me the key.

If I really cared . . .
I would love you anyhow;
But I would ask for the best that you can give
And gently draw it from you.

If I really cared . . .
I would put away my scripts,
And leave my solutions at home.
The performances would end.
We'd be ourselves.

Kinder Words Were Never Spoken

I could tell the minute he walked in the door that it had been a long day. Even his eyes looked tired. I knew there was nothing I could do except take his briefcase and reach out to him with a hug.

I felt my own inner disarray, my physical and emotional fatigue. Sunrise to sunset activities had drained my reserve, and the day's demands were still far from over. Evening chores loomed above me like an impossible mountain: children to supervise; dinner to prepare for tomorrow's company; a house to clean; a lesson to plan for a morning class.

Now, standing before me, was my exhausted husband who had spent all his energy controlling his own twelve-hour day. His favorite easy chair stood waiting for him by the fireplace, the day's newspaper still folded nearby. *He deserves that chair, that fireplace, that paper,* I thought. *He's given more than his share. It's not his fault that the things on my list haven't gotten done.*

He hung his coat in the closet and exchanged his shoes for slippers. Then, rolling up his sleeves, he walked into the pumpkin-pie clutter of the kitchen.

"Been a long day." He yawned and stretched his arms wearily. Then, as though moved by some inner strength, he said, "Now, tell me what I can do for you."

His statement spread like a soothing ointment over the commotion of my day. I couldn't remember ever hearing kinder words. Not "Call me if you need me," or even "Let me know if I can do anything," but "What can I do for you?"—a genuine offer to help!

As I looked into Mark's tired but willing face, I saw a representation of the One who said He had "not come to be served, but to serve . . ." (Mark 10:45). Those words were spoken by the Son of God on a day when His disciples needed a proper perspective on servanthood (10:36) and when a blind man cried out for mercy (10:51).

The Son of God, surrounded by endless requests and wearied by miles of walking, looked *need* squarely in the face and asked, "What do you want Me to do for you?" No claim to His easy chair or thirty minutes with the daily paper by a peaceful fireside. Instead, He saw the burden another carried and offered to help with the load.

In a day when *servanthood* is dying for lack of examples and we get all tied up in theological knots over even the meaning of the word, we might do well to start where Jesus did–with a simple question, "What can I do for you?" Who knows? Those words might revolutionize our marriages as well as our relationships with our children and friends.

Once There Was a Good Samaritan

Once upon a time, in the spring of the year, when trees turn a feathery green and buds begin to force their way out of branches, a Samaritan traveled down a road from one city to another. She was a good Samaritan—warm and sensitive to the needs of others, always willing to come to the aid of someone who hurt.

It was not unusual, therefore, that when the Samaritan came upon a bruised and battered form lying beside the road, she stopped to offer assistance. She felt great sympathy for the wounded victim and gently took her to the nearest place of safety.

That night she listened for a long time to the sorrowful events of the bruised and battered. The Samaritan saw loneliness on her face, heard calls for help. She determined then and there that she would cancel her plans indefinitely in order to minister to the needs of the injured.

With great intensity she threw herself into the task of restoring the wounded. She listened, prayed, and encouraged. By and by, a strange thing began to take place.

Gradually, quietly, scenes from her patient's unfortunate life became so real in her mind that she began to feel the hurts herself. Night after night she went to bed exhausted, dreaming lonely dreams and hearing calls for help. Her resources were nearly drained, and she began to wonder why she saw so little progress in her patient. After all, she thought, I am faithfully bearing another's burdens, as the Lord of the kingdom commanded me to do.

One day when she felt she could bear the load no longer, the Lord of the kingdom passed her way and saw the strain on her body. "Put down the load, My child," He said. "I want you to carry one another's burdens, not absorb them. I alone am strong enough to do that."

The good Samaritan cried tears of relief. Realizing she could not, and was not expected to, carry forever another's load as well as her own, she returned to her patient. "I've given you what I can," she said. "Now I must move on."

The good Samaritan went on her way. But her thoughts return now and then to the wounded form found beside the road that spring day. Now, whenever she comes upon one who's fallen, she stops to lift that person up. But she does so without allowing the injured one's burden to cause her to stumble too.

I know. I was that good Samaritan.

Priority Mail

YOU COME TO ME
In words
Written on yellow sheets of
Notebook paper
Inked in blue
Folded and stuffed
In a plain, white envelope

Lots of letters
Come and go
In my post office box
But only one
Matters
The one that brings
You
To me

I know the writing
Tear open the seal
Time stops
Even people wait

PRIORITY MAIL

There is just
You
And me
And the letter

I find a place without people
A solitary spot under a birch tree
To read about
You
And me
And us

I belong to those words
To the one who penned
The neat block letters
I look for you behind the lines
Where are you as you write?
What are your feelings?
What are your thoughts?
What were you doing
Before you wrote?
What will you do
When you are done?

I look for meaning
I read between the lines
In search of
Your love
In search of
The you that I love
I read again
The same words
But new information
Four times
Over the yellow pages
With blue block letters
And I've missed half of lunch
But nothing matters
Except
You are here with me
In words

TENDERNESS

Delivered in a twenty-cent envelope
That seems like gold

BUT IMAGINE:
An unopened letter
From the one
You love

IMAGINE:
Unread correspondence
From the God
You love

Thy King Cometh

Darkness settled in around me as our car coasted to a silent stop on the shoulder of the expressway. In a steady stream of purring motors and glowing headlights, Christmas Eve passed by us. All in a hurry. Off to a glad celebration of family and friends. Lights in the dark. A promise of hope. Only to fade into red glows disappearing down Interstate 55.

The warm splendor of city lights rising from the distant horizon made us even more aware of our dilemma. There were no lights in our car. They had died with the motor. Inside and out, all was cold, dark, and silent.

At least we were on the safe side of the city, where Cadillac Sevilles and Suburban station wagons moved in and out of the night. Soon one would stop to help us.

But all that stopped was a pickup truck that sounded like a piece of earth-moving equipment. It ground to a halt behind us. From the other side of the city, the wrong side. I reached over and locked both doors.

"Come on. We have a ride," Mark said. He helped me into the cab of the truck, which was little more than a heap of rust held together by two doors and a floor. Dust. Dirt. Bottles. Unkempt. Unclean. Heavy smell of alcohol.

Three hours later the couple still hovered over us like angels sent to guard. They followed the truck with our car in tow to the garage, hung around until the repairs were made, led us back onto the Interstate, then tooted their final farewell. And somewhere in the night two of a different kind went on about their business of Christmas Eve while we headed home to celebrate with family.

Thy King cometh. Not in Cadillac Sevilles or Suburban station wagons. But in drafty pick-up trucks that vibrate the earth when they move. Thy King cometh. In gold, frankincense, and myrrh, laid in the dust before deity's child. For the message of Christmas, the true message of Christmas, is that Majesty came, wrapped itself in swaddling clothes, and stabled itself in hay. Behold, thy King cometh unto thee.

Listen to the tender moments of your life.
What do you hear?

CHAPTER NINE

Commitments and Covenants

Human Dilemmas

No one wants to talk
They are lost in private cubicles
Mainliner magazine
Yellow notebook pads
Documents
Data
Seatbelts
And sometimes sleep.
Row 11. Seat E.
I settle in. In fact,
I don't want to talk either.
I'm glad the man next to me
Is reading The Wall Street Journal.
That way I don't have to tell him
Where I've been
Where I'm going
And what I do for a living.
Besides,
It's hard to talk
Against the roar of the engines.
Cubicles are easier. Safer.
Safer
Until the warning bell . . .
"Did he say 'the warning bell'?"
"Aborted take-off . . ."
The pilot has spoken.
The giant bird sits lifeless
At the end of the runway.
Engines silenced.
Someone say something.

Tell us it's okay.
How about another plane?
Another flight?
Another anything.
In our nervousness we wait.
And in our wait
We reach over the walls of silence
To find another human,
Someone else whose palms are sweaty,
Someone else who is thinking
Home
Family
And why did I ever choose this flight?
Suddenly words flow freely.
There are no strangers on this flight.
We are closed up together
In uncertainty—uncertainty that
Locks us in conversation
About where we've been
Where we'd like to go
And what we do for a living.
All the way to Minneapolis
We talk
Drawing support
For our faltering courage
Comfort for the
Uncertain sounds and the
Unusual take-off
Relief from
Warning bells
Fears
And isolated cubicles.

Human dilemmas—
They dissolve silence
And, if we let them
They draw us together
They draw us to the God
Who understands human dilemmas.

The Viking Cowboy

"When does a job become more important than the people you love?" As a Christian concerned about God's priorities for my life, I've often asked that question. In an unexpected way, I met my answer.

His ten-gallon hat barely cleared the doorway as he boarded Flight 721 in St. Louis. As he moved his towering frame down the aisle, swung his genuine cowhide case into the overhead compartment, and eased into the seat next to mine, I could tell this was no ordinary cowboy.

He was as cool and masculine as any aftershave commercial. He knew all the right lines and used them generously on everyone around him. I buried myself in my *Mainliner* magazine and tried not to notice. I wasn't enamored with a cowboy who appeared to have an ego twice the size of his hat. And I wasn't about to fall for his act.

"That a good article?" his voice boomed in my direction.

"Uh-huh."

"Ever heard of the Minnesota Vikings? I play football for them."

Something in his tone sounded haunting. I sensed there was more he wanted to say. I closed my magazine and listened. He glanced across the aisle, then back at me. No one was watching. He quit acting.

"Golden boy. Down the tubes." As he motioned thumbs down, I noticed his ring with an NFL insignia.

"See these eyes? They're red from crying. Just left my wife and two sons. Can't even be with them anymore. Kicked out of my own house. Didn't know football players cried, did you?"

As the 727 roared toward Chicago, he spilled out the pieces of his broken dream. Hard work. Irregular schedules. Frequent moves. Always the excuse that someday they would have time for each other. But one day there was no more someday.

"You know what my job became?" he asked. "An ego trip, that's what! After a while, my job was everything. Couldn't even hear what my family was saying.

"You write articles. Tell your readers that when a job makes you deaf to your family, you'd better *quit.* Tell 'em I said so—and I ought to know!"

We pulled up to the United gate, but even the congestion on Concourse E didn't interrupt the cowboy's discourse. "You've got your family," he exclaimed. "Hang on to them for all you're worth. Make them feel they're the most important thing to you. It's an empty world without them. I ought to know."

He tipped his ten-gallon hat in my direction, and I watched him climb into his waiting limousine and head for downtown Chicago. *Tomorrow,* I thought, *he'll be back running touchdowns.*

"Tell your readers," he'd said to me, "when your job makes you deaf to your family, you'd better quit." I promised him I would.

Partners in Covenant

I could tell by the way she twirled her wedding ring and tapped her coffee mug with her spoon that she had something important on her mind.

"Well, Ruth," she began, "our love is dead. There's nothing there anymore. After ten years of being married to him, about all I feel is that I have a *friend.* I can't go on living with a man I don't love."

Her words did not surprise me. Her happiness had vanished like the last rays of a setting sun. I knew she was contemplating divorce. *Why remain married when love has died?*

Since that talk with Amy, I've thought long and hard about love and marriage and have decided that marriage is not only a matter of love but of will as well. My heart does not determine its success or failure; my head does. Oneness is a choice I make, not something I feel.

But I live in a world of sentimentality. The media clamors for my heart, not my head. It teaches me to feel, but not always to think. It paints happiness with sunsets and roses. Sells love in a red velvet valentine. Promises intimacy in a bottle from Paris. And when the sunsets fade and the rose petals fall, the forces around me say: "Look for other sunsets, other roses. There is no reason to continue . . ."

Except one—the covenant I made. A rational agreement. Not a conditional commitment that changes with circumstances. A promise to be kept whether or not the warm fuzzy feelings last.

Sometimes Mark forgets that I need the car on Wednesday. And sometimes he tracks mud or snow on my freshly waxed floor. But we are still *partners* in a covenant. I decide to love, to overlook, to forgive and forget. Not because these things come naturally for me, but because I know forgiving will make it easier for us to keep our promise to each other.

How well I remember when Mark and I bought our first house. We knew it was perfect for us and were convinced God had directed. Boldly we paid our earnest money, signed the contract, bound ourselves legally to that house. Our money had spoken.

But the aftermath was emotional. What if we'd made the wrong decision? What if things got tough and the money wasn't there? What if we found defects in the house? What if we outgrew it? What if another house would have been better?

We *could* back out—except we'd signed and sealed the agreement with cash. The investment was too high. The cost of pulling out was too great. There was no turning back. Our wills held us to the monetary commitment we had made.

Although buying a house is a far cry from a lifetime commitment to marriage, I suggest that if we have learned to honor commitments as temporary as buying a house, perhaps it's time we apply the principle to commitments as permanent as marriage.

To Have or To Hold?

"Want to know the two most important things parents can do for their teenagers?" asked a silver-haired father of four grown children. "Trust them and let them go. You remember that someday when you have teenagers."

He was a stranger to me—a casual conversationalist at a social event. But I had the feeling his advice was worth remembering; soon I would be the parent of a teenager.

Today I read about a parent from a different time and place and recalled the advice of the silver-haired stranger.

In response to Pharoah's edict, "No more Hebrew boy babies!" this mother tried a daring plan. A basket lined with tar and pitch, papyrus reeds as camouflage, the waters of the mighty Nile, her baby son—and the daughter she trusted.

This Hebrew mother knew that supervising a dramatic

escape was adult business. It called for quick thinking, wise action, and stable emotions. She understood the perils her daughter would face, but she trusted her daughter and she trusted God.

After placing her son in the basket, she deposited it among the reeds and stationed her daughter beside the river on standby alert. Then she went home to attend her duties of the day, leaving the fate of baby Moses with Miriam, a young girl about the age of my twelve-year-old Jori.

As Jori grows older I hope I will remember the young Hebrew girl whose mother had enough confidence in her to trust her to make life-and-death decisions for her infant brother. With that kind of affirmation from a parent, it is little wonder that Miriam grew up to be one of Israel's great leaders.

"Trust them and let them go," the stranger advised. And in his advice I discovered another of God's amazing paradoxes. To keep your teenagers, you must let them go.

Nicky unknowingly illustrated the truth one day while blowing soap bubbles in the backyard.

"Don't try to hold on to the bubbles," Nicky directed his guests in typical eight-year-old fashion. "That's how they go away."

He balanced a colorful giant bubble in the palm of his hand to demonstrate. The delicate sphere swayed gently with the breeze, but remained securely in his hand.

"See," he explained, closing his fingers, "if you try to grab it, you lose it."

And the bubble was gone.

In the silent explosion of Nicky's soap bubble the stranger's advice regarding children came back to me: "Trust them—and let them go."

Easy Commitment

Commitment was always an abstract term to me until I saw it demonstrated one day at an airport in Colombia, South America.

At 9:00 A.M. steam was already rising from the parched red clay. As we drove through the gate toward the concrete square that seemed to squat in the middle of nowhere, we realized this was no ordinary day at the Cúcuta airport. Lines of green school buses clogged the parking area, and the entire town seemed to be moving *en masse* toward the terminal. Not a suitcase was in sight.

The activities at the Cúcuta airport that day appeared to have nothing whatever to do with travel. For those of us trying to go somewhere, a seven-hour wait began.

We threaded our way through the human barricades of green army fatigues, pushed past bayonets and billy clubs, and asked if there was a plane going to Miami.

"*El presidente* is coming," was the response we got. "No planes." Bands played, people yelled, banners fluttered. Everyone seemed caught up in the excitement, but not everyone in the crowd was cordial.

"Dissidents," we were told, as we watched the angry mob from behind the safety of glass doors. "Angry at their poverty. They want *el presidente* to know."

That day I saw a living demonstration of commitment. A young woman dissident held the restless crowd in her power as she waved a red flag. Her dark eyes blazed, and her long hair switched wildly as she oscillated from place to place like a fan on high speed. The sun poured down its 104-degree rays, and the air was motionless.

Inside the terminal we munched our sandwiches and drank ice cold Cokes. Outside, in the broiling noon-day heat, stood the woman of commitment. No lunch break or shade for her. Sweat ran down her face as she pounded the air with her fists. Her audience cheered.

Seven hours later her mission was accomplished. Her *presidente* had heard. The military pushed the all-day demonstration back into the waiting buses, and once again the Cúcuta airport became a place of transportation.

As we lifted off that clay oven, still steaming at four o'clock in the afternoon, I thought of how much my commitment to Christ costs me. A commitment served on padded pews in an air-conditioned sanctuary with people I enjoy seeing once a week! Can I even call it commitment if it doesn't cost me something?

Listen to the commitments and covenants in your life. What do you hear?

CHAPTER TEN

Mountains and Monuments

Rooted

Life is full of forces,
Forces that make me like a blade of grass—
dried
detached
carried along by a breeze.
Its direction depends on the wind.
It rests for awhile
until the next gust comes along
and carries it somewhere else;
no direction
no weight of its own
completely at the mercy of
outside forces.

God, I need inside force.
Give me whatever it takes
to make a tree stand:
the sap that makes it live
the roots that keep it anchored
no matter how hard the wind is blowing.

Show me the rivers
where I can put my roots down deep.
Give me the courage of a tree
And not just a blade of dried grass.

Some Thoughts on Monuments

Not even a whisper could be heard in the vast cathedral with its towering arches and translucent domes. A sacred silence hung over the marble pillars, draped the golden altar, and muted the velvet and mother-of-pearl.

In the middle of downtown Maracaibo, Venezuela, surrounded by dusty streets, fruit vendors, barking dogs, and painted stucco, man had created his altar of worship to God. I stood amazed at the ability to create so delicate a balance of order and beauty.

As I left the cathedral in Maracaibo that day, I thought of other altars—formal and informal—built as memorials to the visitation of God. Altars built by Noah, Abraham, Isaac, Jacob, and Moses. Pilgrims and strangers. People in transit. They had survival to think of, tents to pitch on the sandy desert floor, herds to tend, families to feed. Yet they built altars. Some were piles of rough, irregular stones and sod collected from the wilds. But each stone was laid with intricate precision and skill. Centuries later, some still remain on the plains of the Middle East.

I also thought of tabernacle altars, defined and specific, blue-printed by God. Acacia wood from the mimosa trees that grew along the Dead Sea. A tough and beautiful orange-and-brown-hued encasement. Overlays of brass, copper, and gold. Four horns and a crown. Prototypes of altars yet to come in Jerusalem—the temples of Solomon and Herod.

These altars, fifteen feet high and thirty feet across, were even more magnificent and impressive than their desert predecessors. The focal point, a tower of bronze surrounded by terraced stairs, represented man's approach to God.

We don't build Old Testament altars anymore. The tables of stone are replicas of the past. They have been replaced "by a new and living way opened for us through the curtain, that is, His body" (Heb. 10:20).

Our altars of worship have deteriorated into a few haphazard moments with God. No beauty. No pleasant fragrance. Just a kind of magical charm to ensure a peaceful day. We leave no monument—no permanent record that on this spot God has spoken. No memorial to His greatness, His love, His care. We leave no record, for often we have not heard His voice above our own chatter.

I think it might not be a bad idea if we'd learn to build altars again—daily, orderly, specific monuments to the fact that God has spoken. In doing so, we might relearn what it means to "worship the Lord in the beauty of holiness" (Psalm 29:2 KJV).

Stepping Out

It's like
jumping into an icy mountain stream
from dry, hot rocks;
rolling out of a warm sleeping bag
into a cold morning;
turning the shower off
and stepping out;
going off the high dive
for the first time;
not reaching for another potato chip;
typing the first word
of the book you are writing;
pushing yourself off a cliff
because there is no other way down.
Trusting God is hard to do.

Blessed Are the Hungry

At first glance nothing about the stately old church appeared out of the ordinary. The white clapboard frame was obviously old, probably dating back to the mid-1800s. The steeple, like all other church steeples, stretched heavenward, pulling my thoughts with it . . . *An infinite God is up there who dwells not only in temples made by hand, but in the sanctuary of my heart.* It was a fortifying thought in the middle of my busy day of travel and meetings.

I pushed open the cast-iron gate and followed the fence around the buildings. Stained glass windows seemed almost lifelike. Figures of the God-Man Jesus. The Bread of Life. The Shepherd of the sheep. The Door. The Vine. The Living Water. The Resurrection and the Life.

Magnificent structure, I thought to myself. In my mind I complimented some pilgrim of the past who had constructed his altar to God.

My first hint that the inside of the structure didn't match the outside was the oak-carved pulpit in the vestibule. Instead of a Bible resting on the ornate fixture, I saw after-dinner mints, a reservation log, and a sign that read, "Welcome to the Sanctuary. Luncheon served: 11:30–2:30. Dinner: 5:00–10:30."

A wide aisle carpeted in red led to the altar. But beneath the majestic arches and gilded organ pipes stood a buffet table. Puffed Mushrooms. Fried Zucchini. Baked French Onion Soup. Julienne Salad. Brochette of Beef.

The organ cubicle had become a bar; the baptistry, a fish tank; and the pews, cozy conversation centers for four.

I surveyed the scene before me and pondered its implications. Houses of worship—the places where we once fed our souls—had been turned into fancy restaurants to fill our stomachs. Where once we came with an appetite for God, we now come with a craving for prime rib and filet mignon.

"Well, that will keep me filled 'til dinner," a jolly man said as he paid the hostess and struggled to button his vest.

I thought of Jesus' words, "Blessed are those who hunger and thirst for righteousness, for they shall be satisfied" (Matt. 5:6 NASB). I returned to my car feeling sad for a society whose need to eat has become more important than its need to worship God.

Christmas Burnout

The December day was brilliant but the mood that followed me up the church stairs was dark. I'd walked here many times before, but today it seemed I was treading on alien turf.

"Ruth, you won't believe it," was all the church secretary said to me as she unlocked the doors, flipped on the light switch, and waited for me to enter. I stared at the ruins before me.

"It all happened in about five hours," she said. "A policeman spotted the smoke about 5:30 in the morning . . ." She reached out and touched a window ledge where a glass hurricane lamp was baked dark brown and a white dove turned blackbird stood with his tail in the air and his head pointed down. "Our Christmas concerts were scheduled to begin on Saturday night. The sanctuary was all decorated."

I moved silently through the blackened shell. *My church doesn't live here anymore.* The thought was like a death knell. We had dedicated both our children under the giant wooden cross that had hung at the front of the sanctuary. Today there was no cross. Instead, massive organ pipes spread out over the choir loft like melted candles.

I walked to the platform where two-year-old Jori had said her first lines in a Sunday school Christmas program. A star had shone overhead and shepherds had walked down the center aisle while the organ played "O Little Town of Bethlehem." Today there was no music. Instead, broken glass and ashes crunched under our feet.

Christmas—swallowed up by a tragic fire. I turned to go, but a white cup among a tangled mass of melted plastic caught my eye. Its whiteness told me it had been placed there since the fire. As I moved closer I saw on it the red shield of the Salvation Army.

"They came early," the secretary said, "and stayed through the day, serving hot coffee and doughnuts, doing whatever they could. We didn't know them. But they came, just to show they cared, I guess."

As we closed the door on the cold, dark sanctuary, I knew that the message of Christmas had been preached from this place after all.

Long ago, the God of the universe came via Bethlehem to visit the charred ash heaps of life. Now I see Him in the lives of people who come to care for the burned out places of my life.

Listen to the mountains and monuments in your life.
What do you hear?

CHAPTER ELEVEN

Passing Time

Looking Back

We were together again.
This time we spent our morning over coffee and
quiche in a little French cafe on Broadway:
South America in review, current projects, life in Manhattan,
people we knew, where do we go from here?
We said good-bye until my next trip east.
I flew homeward but thought backward—
Did I talk too much? Say the right things?
Take the conversation only where I wanted it to go?
Unwrap more of myself to her than I should have?
Was I witty? Sincere? Interesting? Caring? Informed?
Will she invite me for brunch next time I'm in New York?
She was someone I liked. Respected. Admired.
It mattered what she thought.
Put the movie on the reel and run it through again. "Beautiful sky we flew through, wasn't it?" He handed me my coat from the overhead compartment. "I'm sure it was." But I really hadn't noticed.

We didn't agree—my nine-year-old daughter and I.
"Everybody else's mother is letting them go . . .
I'll be the only one . . . the odd ball . . . always the odd ball."
Exchange of words: Thoughtful. Calm. Firm.
Discussion ended . . . then resurfaced,
This time to create waves—
Tidal waves that capsized any hopes for rational conversation.
She slammed the door. Off to school in the eye of the storm.
I moved on with my day but relived the storm.
Was I too harsh? Too narrow? Too protective?
Did I react rather than act? Push her too far?
Leave my fingerprints all over the image she had of herself?

Stuff her back inside her hide-away shell?
She was at a delicate age. Fragile ego.
Balancing on a precarious perch.
It mattered how I treated her.
Put the movie on the reel and run it through again.
"What did you do today?" he asked as he sat his briefcase down in the front hall and gave me a hug. "Well, I . . . I thought a lot. Funny I should be so tired."

The performance had ended. Lights turned off.
They closed the door. I kept it open.
Instant replay of the scene.
Was it too long? I forgot to set my watch.
Enough illustrations? I wish I'd used another one.
Left out point number three. Good point, too.
Meant to say . . . I think it came out something else.
Did I talk about what they feel? What do they feel?
Should have asked more questions beforehand.
People judge you on your finished product . . .
Grade you on performance.
It matters how I do.
Put the movie on the reel and run it through again. "Enjoyed your talk. Learned a lot," The monogrammed notecard said. Strange she should feel that way about my failure.

Lord, when I say good-bye to friends,
Help me think about them and forget about me.

When I discipline my children,
Help me do what I need to do and spend the rest of the day on other things.

When I finish a talk,
Help me close the door and leave it behind.

Don't let me go through life facing backward.

When Old Is Young

Uncle Alton wasn't really all that young. In fact, he told me he was somewhere around ninety-two or ninety-three. But in some ways, Uncle Alton was the youngest man I ever knew.

He wasn't really my uncle, or anyone else's uncle except Christine's, but for miles around he was everybody's uncle. After I stopped by to visit him on that hot day in August, I knew why.

The minute I knocked on the wooden screen door, he appeared, shuffling toward me in his bright blue shirt and Osh-Kosh bib overalls. I'd never seen a spryer shuffle.

"Come in. Come in. S'glad to see ye. Glad to see ye." His eyes were wide sparkles of blue that matched his shirt. His mouth was on the verge of laughter. In fact, his whole face looked like laughter—a look that didn't fade even after I'd been there for an hour.

I had come to see Christine, but Uncle Alton automatically became my host. He asked how I was, set the oscillating fan in my direction, and quietly called Christine in from the kitchen.

His eyes never shifted into a stare, and he never went to sleep. He followed every word with great interest, nodding his head vigorously when he agreed or remembered the event we were discussing.

Uncle Alton was all color. When I asked about the past, he talked about it. He recreated the days of mule wagons as he told how he had run the muddy ruts of the road in front of the house. He told about the sugar caning he had done with a team of horses harnessed to a revolving log that served as a press. But he seemed much more interested in the present—in the patch of watermelons he was watching over, in the deep purple hydrangea that was blooming just outside his window, or in the tiny hummingbirds he fed each morning. He teased Christine about forgetting to water his morning glories.

"The joy of my life," Christine nodded in his direction. "Always teasing and always listening to tapes."

As I passed his tape deck on my way out I saw his collection—"Studies of the Beatitudes," "1 and 2 Peter," "Sermons from the Psalms," "Daniel and Revelation."

The secret of youth, I thought to myself. "They that wait upon the Lord, shall renew their strength. They shall mount up with wings as eagles. They shall run and not be weary. They shall walk and not faint" (Isaiah 40:31 KJV). I could almost see Uncle Alton with eagle's wings.

Personal Dividends

As a sophomore in high school, I never stopped to think where my words—and God's—might take someone else. But there they were in an old friend, standing right before my eyes at a get-acquainted time for new faculty wives like myself. My husband Mark was starting a new career as a seminary professor.

Peggy's presence at the retreat was no surprise. I knew her husband had joined the seminary faculty following several pastorates. But when I saw how God was using her to lead a committee of faculty wives that day, I was suddenly transported to long ago and far away.

Twenty-three years before and 850 miles away we had been tenth-graders together. There had been more differences than similarities between us then.

Peggy had lived near that small Pennsylvania town all her life. I was a transplant from the cotton fields of

Alabama. I had come to school with a blue plaid hand-me-down skirt. Peggy wore Pendleton wools. She swam in her backyard pool, rode her horse every Saturday, and had traveled in Europe. It hadn't been our similarities that drew us together.

Nor had it been any outward evidence of need. Peggy was surrounded by friends. She appeared to have all the personality, looks, money, and stability she could possibly desire. Nor had there been any great crisis in either of our lives to drive us together.

But there had been a slow, steady undercurrent of interest in each other's lives: I asked for tips on the game of tennis, which she played like a pro; I called to find out about her dad's back surgery; Peggy wanted to know about the little country church my father had pastored in Alabama and about the Christian club I went to every Tuesday after school.

We talked about things that were important to us—French, boys, teachers, parents, God. . . . A personal God was a new thought to Peggy. Her eyes wouldn't leave my face when I'd tell her how sure I was that God not only lived in heaven, but that He also lived in those of us who believed in Him on earth.

Peggy knew God had moved into my activities, my attitudes, and my dreams for the future. "He's not pushy," I explained. "It's up to you. Someday, when you're ready, God will meet you."

Now, twenty-three years later, I saw living proof that God's Word, both silent and spoken, never misses its mark. Faithfully invested in a ready heart, it will yield dividends!

Coming Home

Twenty-five years, and I'm coming home—down the joyous roads of my childhood. Today we take the narrow, two-lane highway that stretches south through endless acres of majestic Alabama white pine. I am lost in the beauty. The simplicity. The tranquility.

I'm coming home; leaving the confusing mass of eight lane traffic, the concrete and steel that futilely reach for the sky, and the people who are always in a hurry to be somewhere else. Alabama. Place of my dreams. Goal for my life. Where people have time to sit on their front porch swings and talk to each other for an afternoon or two. Where white frame houses stand strong and neat; where pecan trees shade the green yards; where white, fleecy cotton blankets the fields; and where the ever-present pine fragrance fills the air. Alabama. Where people work hard, never have a lot, but always enough. Where neighbor means everyone within a fifty-mile radius. Where someone always takes time to fix you a dinner of hot biscuits, black-eyed peas, and chicken in dumplings. Alabama. Why have I stayed away so long?

The road goes on, but we stop; dreams suddenly freeze into reality. The white frame house is yellow with age, and an old man in overalls is asleep on the steps. A ripped screen hangs loose from the corner of my bedroom window. No pecan trees shade the house anymore, and the front yard is a rusted-out relic of old bottles, cans, hay rake, and a car with all four tires and its insides missing. The porch swing is gone and half the porch with it. There are no fleecy fields of cotton beyond, only weeds. The lumber company has long since stripped the woods of its pine.

My neighbor who loved to fix me black-eyed peas and biscuits and always called me her "Black-eyed Ruth Ann," sits and stares at me with vacant eyes. I don't think she remembers.

"She doesn't even want to get out of bed anymore," her daughter tells me. Mary's kitchen is silent.

I close the door to Mary's house and sadly climb back into our Pontiac with its Illinois license plates.

"Why were the old days better than these?" the biblical writer asked. "It is not wise to ask such questions" (Ecc. 7:10). Mark starts the car and we head north in silence. I am thankful for my past, but in that brief backward glance, I also found contentment in my present. I am ready to move ahead.

Listen to the passing of time in your life.
What do you hear?